DOUG BATCHELOR

Who do you think you are?

Pacific Press® Publishing Association
Nampa, Idaho
Oshawa, Ontario, Canada
www.pacificpress.com

Cover design by Gerald Lee Monks
Cover design resources from dreamstime.com
Inside design by Aaron Troia

Copyright © 2010 by Pacific Press® Publishing Association
Printed in the United States of America
All rights reserved

Unless otherwise noted, all Scriptures are quoted from The New King
James Version, copyright © 1979, 1980, 1982, Thomas Nelson, Inc.,
Publishers.

Scripture quotations marked KJV are from the King James Version.

Scripture texts credited to NRSV are from the New Revised Standard
Version of the Bible, copyright © 1989 by the Division of Christian
Education of the National Council of the Churches of Christ in the
USA. Used by permission. All rights reserved.

You can obtain additional copies of this book by calling toll-free 1-800-
765-6955 or by visiting http://www.adventistbookcenter.com.

ISBN 13: 978-0-8163-2415-6
ISBN 10: 0-8163-2415-8

10 11 12 13 14 • 5 4 3 2 1

Table of Contents

Dedicated to my God, my family,
and my church—the things that last.

Introduction
Identity Theft

William and Jackie Parker,* both successful New York City advertising professionals, were puzzled when they began to notice some unusual expenses on their bank statements. Their perplexity was resolved when they went to their upscale vacation home on Long Island. They found that another couple had been living in their home for six weeks. Posing as friends of the Parkers, these strangers had been enjoying the good life—eating the Parkers' food and spending their money. They had managed to access the Parkers' funds from the bank documents and other personal information they found in the home. The couple even escaped in the Parkers' spare car, which they had been using the whole time.

Margaret Murray, a South Carolina homemaker, tried in vain for months to get her bank to close a fraudulent checking account that had been opened in her name after her driver's license was stolen. Instead, Murray was arrested at her home in front of her son on thirteen warrants stemming from bad checks. She had to make several court appearances in two counties to clear her name. She felt her good reputation had been hijacked by some invisible enemy.

These troubling stories are a small example of what has become a crime epidemic in North America—identity theft.

*Fictitious names.

That's what happens when someone wrongfully obtains another person's personal data and uses it for his or her own economic gain. In the wrong hands, your personal information—especially your Social Security number, bank account or credit card numbers, or telephone calling card personal identification number (PIN)—can be terribly abused.

Abraham Abdallah perpetrated one of the most blatant instances of identity theft. In February of 2002, the New York Police Department arrested him, accusing him of committing that crime on a massive scale. This thirty-two-year-old busboy, a high school dropout, is suspected of stealing the identities of Steven Spielberg, George Lucas, Oprah Winfrey, Ted Turner, and scores of other famous people whose names he got from a *Forbes* magazine list of wealthy Americans. Abdallah had bought a machine that makes credit cards and used it to make his own credit cards—with other people's names on them. At the time of his arrest, he had eight hundred such credit cards and had access to billions of dollars that belonged to other people.[1]

Every day, thousands of people report that funds are stolen from their accounts. In the worst cases, criminals completely take over someone's identity, run up vast debts, and commit crimes, leaving the victims with destroyed credit and sometimes even a criminal record. Sadly, when the victims discover what's happened, it can take years and small fortunes to get their records cleared.

As devastating as this kind of identity theft is, there's another kind that's far worse! It's the ultimate example of reputation robbery, and it can be seen in the world around us every day. Satan hijacked the good name of God, and then, after claiming God's titles, he seized His earthly creation and went on an unprecedented global crime spree in which he multiplied sin, pain, and misery on a scale that we can't even begin to comprehend. On top of this, Satan then carefully devised a plot to shift the responsibility for all the evil that he has caused onto the Creator, to make Him bear the cost.

God's response? He consented to pay the ultimate price to clear His name—He sent His beloved Son to die.

Here is the central focus of this book: Satan and his minions are out to steal the spiritual identity of God's children. He is seeking to confuse and deceive believers regarding who they really are in God so they have no hope or peace. Throughout history, he has done this with a frightening level of success. Scripture says "the great dragon . . . that serpent of old, called the Devil and Satan, . . . deceives the whole world" (Revelation 12:9).

Faith is the key ingredient in the recipe of salvation. "Without faith it is impossible to please" God (Hebrews 11:6). Knowing this, the devil is constantly causing Christians everywhere to doubt their identities—to doubt their new birth, to doubt the validity of their adoption, and to doubt the position, the possessions, and the power God has conferred upon them as His redeemed children. Millions struggle to embrace the truth of what they can become through faith in Christ. It is essentially an identity problem. People don't know who they are in Jesus.

Because of the sacrifice of Christ, we need to view ourselves, by faith, differently than we would otherwise. We are born again as new creatures with a new heart, a new name, a new peace, and a new mission. When we can truly accept the profound revelation that we receive a new identity in Jesus, our experience will be radically revolutionized. The apostle Paul counsels us, as he did the believers in Ephesus, to "be renewed in the spirit of your mind, and . . . put on the new man which was created according to God, in true righteousness and holiness" (Ephesians 4:23, 24).

---

1. BBC News, "Dish Washer 'Cleaned Up in Internet Fraud,' " *BBC News,* http://news.bbc.co.uk/2/hi/business/1231825.stm.

Chapter 1
Identity Crisis

Do you not know yourselves, that Jesus Christ is in you?

—2 Corinthians 13:5

A number of years ago, famed author Edgar Rice Burroughs wrote a book about a missionary couple working in an African jungle. The couple was killed, but amazingly, their baby survived and was "adopted." A mother gorilla, still pining for her own baby that had died recently, took the little human baby and cared for him tenderly. In the story, this baby manages to survive and is raised in the jungle by these great apes, living as one of them. Eventually, this wild man is discovered by other humans, but he thinks he's a gorilla, so he has to be taught not to behave like one. You know his name—Tarzan, of course.

That fiction classic was based upon some stories rooted in truth. There have been at least two or three cases of feral children who lived among, or were even adopted and cared for by, wild animals. In the late eighteenth century, there was a boy who lived among the wolves that roamed in the woods of Lacaune in southern France. This boy, who was called the "wild child," was running on all fours when he was captured. The people who cared for him were never really able to teach him to speak or to act like a human. He had spent so much of his formative years among wolves that he thought he was one of them and never completely got over that idea.

In Africa, a boy, later named John, was found living with a family of monkeys. He was rescued, and though he was developmentally impaired, the missionaries who adopted him did manage to teach him to speak. Later, they discovered he had a beautiful voice, and he began singing. But when someone is raised with animals, it's really hard to teach them that they're human. People have a hard time handling the shock of discovering that they're not even the same species they thought they were.

So here's the big question, a very important one, Who do you think you are—in God?

We aren't merely animals. "God created man in His own image; in the image of God He created him; male and female He created them" (Genesis 1:27). Yet because of distorted self-perception, most people allow their carnal natures to control them. We need to see ourselves through God's eyes. That perspective can make a great deal of difference as to how we view ourselves and how we behave. It can go a long way toward removing the basic insecurity that so many feel. It can ensure that, whatever thieves might do with our credit cards or Social Security numbers, our true identities are forever secure in Jesus Christ.

Accident or design?

Anyone following the news lately is aware of the ongoing debate raging over creation and evolution. In a sense, it's a little bit like the Tarzan story. Are we all really just smart apes—glorified gorillas that have learned to read and to build space stations? Or are we something infinitely nobler? People who think that their existence is just the chance result of billions of years of evolution will have a very different sense of identity than they'd have if they believed they're a unique species, deliberately created in the image of an intelligent and loving God. Believing in intelligent design as opposed to chance evolution will have a profound impact on our self-concepts and what we consider to be the ultimate purpose for our lives. Our sense of who we are is always firmly connected with our understanding of where we came from. Not understanding our divine origin can have a catastrophic negative impact on our life and on the world.

Touring the Nazi concentration camp at Dachau is an experience people don't forget. A friend who visited that place said that before the tour began, the tour guide referred to Charles Darwin and evolution and drew a direct line between the Holocaust and the idea that human beings are merely products of natural selection. If you think about it, that connection makes sense. After all, if the survival of the fittest weeds out inferior specimens, why shouldn't people help the process of evolution along through genocide?

Staggering complexity

Evidence continues to mount that the only reasonable explanation for the origin of life is that life is the product of an intelligent, miraculous work. In the mid-1800s, when Charles Darwin wrote his theory of evolution, many scientists believed in something called spontaneous generation—the idea that living things can spontaneously arise from nonliving material. No doubt they had observed worms and maggots apparently springing forth from decaying meat and fruit. But in 1859, the great scientist Louis Pasteur proved that spontaneous generation doesn't happen. He demonstrated that when decaying material is covered, so flies and other insects don't have access to it, no larvae grow on it. And modern science has made it even clearer that life is extremely complex and can arise only from pre-existing life. This is why the best efforts of evolutionary scientists haven't been able to produce a single living cell—even in expensive, high-tech laboratories.

Twenty-first-century microscopes have enabled scientists to see that even the simplest and smallest organisms are in effect virtual factories, containing thousands of exquisitely designed pieces of intricate molecular machinery; they're far more complicated than the International Space Station. In fact, functionally, each microscopic cell is as complex as a city!

Imagine, if you will, downtown New York City during rush hour. Subways roaring. Elevators whizzing up and down skyscrapers. Taxi cabs . . . well . . . idling in traffic. People striding in and out of buildings, over bridges, and across streets. From ten stories below street level to 180 stories above, it's a dynamo of activity and a complex network of plumbing, electrical, and telecommunications systems. But according to most evolutionary scientists, a single living human cell is staggeringly more complex than New York City at rush hour. "Each of those 100 trillion cells [in a human being] functions like a walled city. Power plants generate the cell's energy. Factories produce proteins, vital units of chemical commerce. Complex transportation systems guide specific chemicals from point to point within the cell. . . . Sentries . . . monitor the outside world for signs of danger. Disciplined biological armies stand ready to grapple with invaders. A centralized genetic government maintains order."[1]

Evolutionists are now playing the alien card. They're saying that a comet or a meteor or alien visitors brought life to our planet. Of course, that theory creates an out-of-this-world argument that is virtually impossible to disprove. Amazingly, in spite of the staggering mountain of evidence that only a miracle could produce life, the modern world refuses to accept the Bible account of creation!

Despite what the evidence makes obvious, much of the modern world teaches that if you believe in the Creation story—that

God simply spoke things into existence—well, you're stupid. You can cheer up; you're in good company. Jesus took Moses' writings as plain truth. He quoted freely from the Old Testament, regarding it as an authority on Creation, the Exodus, and the Flood. He never suggested that any part of Genesis was a parable or a fable. No matter what the world thinks of us, we should believe what Jesus believed.

Evidence of God

There are many sources of evidence for the existence of God. His Word, of course, is the most reliable. But God also reveals Himself to us through other people and through the things He has made. Isaiah 6:3 tells us that angelic creatures in the presence of God called out, "The whole earth is full of His glory!" But many people can't see the Lord through the things He has made because the cataracts of evolution have obscured their vision.

Dr. Lolita Simpson, a friend of mine, walked up to me one day and said, "Doug, I want to show you something. See this flower?"

I thought, *Isn't this sweet. This dear old saint is going to show me a flower!*

But then Dr. Simpson showed the flower to me through the eyes of a scientist. She said, "Here you see five petals, and they're surrounded by five leaves, and inside are five little stems and the stigma and the stamen. And it's all perfectly symmetrical. There's mathematical organization. There's design, beauty, and fragrance too. This could never happen by accident."

Design, organization, and plans don't arise from chaos. That would be like suggesting you could throw a bomb into a junkyard and get a space shuttle when the dust settled—or that you could throw a grenade into a print shop and get the *Encyclopaedia Britannica*!

Biological burps

One of the major struggles I had in accepting Christ, and the Bible in particular, was that I grew up believing in evolution. Virtually all the schools I attended taught that people are nothing more than a highly developed strain of monkeys and that the evolutionary processes took millions and billions of years. Surprisingly, some of the schools where this was taught were religious schools! But if we all evolved from a primeval puddle of mud somewhere, and if we simply disintegrate into fertilizer when we die, then life really has no grand purpose. I believe this false teaching of evolution is largely responsible for the high rate of suicide among teenagers. What can we expect if we tell them life is nothing more than a biological burp?

I'm convinced that people's concepts of who we are and where we came from is affected by our environment—by the things that surround us. Growing up in a big city like New York, I constantly heard the roar of traffic and the scream of sirens. Wherever I turned, I saw concrete, glass, flashing lights, and other man-made things. Mesmerized by the sights and sounds of humanity, I put my trust in people. And since people were telling me we just evolved, I believed it.

I remember asking the science teacher in one of the schools I attended, "Where did the world come from?" In essence, he told me that the sun exploded and sent out a pinwheel of planets and moons, which became our solar system. Even this is incredible when you consider the vastly different composition of the planets and moons in our solar system and that they rotate in different directions.

Next, I asked my teacher, "Where did the sun come from?"

He said the sun came from another big bang. Two gas masses collided and exploded, forming the Milky Way galaxy.

And then I asked, "Where did these gas particles come from?"

Ultimately, even scientists have to acknowledge that something has always existed.

Then, as a teenager, I spent about a year living in a cave, high in some desert mountains outside of Palm Springs, California. In the midst of those majestic mountains, I began to get a whole different perspective on life. There, I was surrounded by cathedral-like canyons, and—you may be surprised—an abundance of life even in what seems to be a sterile desert. For a year I beheld only the things that God made, and that environment had a profound influence on me. It was a lot easier for me to believe in a Divine Creator when I was surrounded by the evidence of His creation.

So we have a choice. We can look at all the miraculous complexity and organization that we observe in the world all around us and believe that it all came from mysterious, mindless gas particles that have always existed and have started exploding, or we can believe that there is an intelligent God, a Creator, who has always existed. I think it is far more logical to believe that our roots go back to a loving, intelligent heavenly Father—and not to nebulous clouds of brainless gas particles that one day happened to collide, then blew up and formed an intricate universe.

However, even if we set aside our faith in God's Word, both reason and science soundly refute evolution. Indeed, mounting scientific evidence indicates that intelligent design stands behind our universe.

The whole world *can* be wrong

When I became a Bible-believing Christian, I didn't check my brain at the church door. I'm still inquisitive about our world and our universe. I still love science. But it wasn't the Bible that convinced me about life's origins. In fact, at first I tried to marry the Bible and evolution. But science and reason kept getting in the way.

As a child, I wanted to be a paleontologist. I could name all the dinosaurs and many of the layers of the geological column. Evolution fascinated me, and I thought people who believed in creation were fools. The evidence was as plain as day, right? It was in the *National Geographic* specials and all those beautifully filmed nature programs on television. All those scientists couldn't be wrong, could they? It was this kind of reasoning that killed Jesus. The people thought, *How can all of our rabbis and scribes and lawyers be wrong and this uneducated Carpenter be right?* But it's human nature to follow the crowd, even when the crowd is clearly in error. That's why the Bible says, "You shall not follow a crowd to do evil" (Exodus 23:2). Yes, that verse is speaking about our actions, but it also covers our philosophies. It doesn't matter if the whole world believes in the theory of evolution; the Bible is our standard of truth. And evolution is totally incompatible with science and with common sense as well as with biblical Christianity.

William James, a founding father of modern psychology, said something to the effect that if you repeat something often enough, some people will believe it, no matter how absurd it is. It seems it's this quirk of human nature that's responsible for people believing the ridiculous idea that, given enough time, chaos will produce order. And now, more and more Christians are being swept up by it, suggesting that God created all the sophisticated design around us using evolutionary processes. But to embrace this compromise also creates an enormous problem: it makes it logically impossible to believe the rest of God's Word is true.

I gradually discovered that the crowd could, in fact, be very wrong—especially if they approach their science with a powerful bias. What is that bias? Please consider the fact that we all have only two choices. Either an intelligent and obviously very powerful God created this universe, or it came into existence by accident—purely through a series of bizarre coincidences. However, if we believe that an intelligent God made all things, then we must also believe that He is the Supreme Authority in the universe and that we must answer to Him. Many people are terrified by the thought that they don't control their destinies and that someday we will all give an account to our Maker for the lives we live. So they are highly motivated, to put it mildly, to remove God from the equation. No God, no accountability.

Darwinism: The evolution of atheism

People who think the Creation story in the book of Genesis is a fairy tale probably won't find much else in that Book to be relevant either. If we don't accept creation as a fact, the other great biblical truths, including God's standards of morality, lose their significance.

Evolution really is the origins myth of atheism. It was developed for the purpose of giving humans the freedom to sin without answering to a higher Power. At its very core, atheism balks at the existence of objective rights and wrongs. Obviously, not all atheists are ready to commit the evil their beliefs allow. Most people are programmed from youth with certain moral restraints. However, to the atheistic evolutionist, humanity has simply evolved into a society that currently frowns on theft and murder; it could just as easily have evolved into something else, and the result couldn't objectively be called good or bad. Thugs could murder till blood ran in the streets, and evolutionists could simply label it as "eliminating the weaker members of the species."

It surprises many that the horrors of the Holocaust find

their underpinnings in the theory of evolution. An examination of Hitler's writings and that of other Nazis reveals that Darwinism heavily influenced the policies of Germany during World War II. In fact, many people are surprised to learn that the entire title of Darwin's book is *On the Origin of Species by Means of Natural Selection, or the Preservation of* Favoured Races *in the Struggle for Life* (emphasis added). Hitler labeled Jews as an inferior race. In fact, he said they were less than human—thereby justifying their torture and murder and the ghastly experiments performed on them in the name of survival of the fittest. And racism continues today because many people believe that some humans are more highly evolved than others. But racism directly contradicts the Bible, which says God "has made from one blood every nation of men to dwell on all the face of the earth" (Acts 17:26).

A false understanding of human origins ultimately degrades society. Consider the nations that have made atheism the core of their culture—the former Soviet Union, Cuba, China, and Vietnam. But exhibit A is the drastic differences between North and South Korea. If you stand on the thirty-eighth parallel, you can see the very bleak and backward existence of the imprisoned people of North Korea. Then you can turn around and look south, toward Seoul, where you'll see a bright, clean, free, civilized society. The core difference? South Korea has religious freedom and is a Christian stronghold, while North Korea teaches evolution and atheism.

Evolutionists can rationalize all kinds of bad behavior as merely part of the evolution of human beings. After all, if we're just animals fulfilling a natural urge, nothing is inherently immoral. As a teenager, I learned that my science teacher slept with a woman in the loft of his home while his pregnant wife was sitting downstairs. Though it deeply hurt his wife, he appeared indifferent to her feelings. He excused himself by saying, "Not all of the primates we've evolved from are monogamous, so adultery is perfectly natural. We can't help it." Evolution clearly undermines moral living.

Who do you think you are? You will act like who you think you are. If you think you're a gorilla or a wolf, well, you'll be prone to act the part. As a Christian, it's crucial that you know—and frequently remind yourself—who you are based on God's definition, not the one that says you're a grown-up monkey. That's why for many people this whole question of creation versus evolution is so important. It's not just an entertaining debate over some obscure scientific issue. No, instead it gets to the heart of the questions of just who we are, why we're here, and how we're to live our lives.

Chemical scum or divine design?

Consider the view of Shakespeare. He wrote, "What a piece of work is man! how noble in reason! how infinite in faculty! in form and moving, how express and admirable! in action, how like an angel! in apprehension, how like a god! the beauty of the world! the paragon of animals!"[2]

Isaac Newton was one of the greatest scientists in all of history—one whose influence is felt even today. Though he was a scientist, Newton was also a devout Christian, and he believed that his research helped people understand the power and majesty of the Creator. Newton is said to have written of his scientific investigations, wrote, "O God! I think thy thoughts after thee!"

Now, jump ahead with me to our day and age. Stephen Hawking is another scientist that many people have heard of. He wrote the book called *A Brief History of Time,* one of the most popular and best-selling books in the past century. At one point, Hawking wrote, "The human race is just a chemical scum on a moderate-sized planet, orbiting round a very average star in the outer suburb of one among a hundreds billion galaxies."[3] What a diametric change! What a total transition in philosophy! One believed in God, and one didn't.

The great theologian Reinhold Niebuhr wrote, "Man has always been his own most vexing problem. How shall he think of himself?"[4] How shall we? The answer is important, because how we view ourselves will influence how we view others, and how we view others will influence how we treat them. If we believe that people are beings made in the image of God, beings for whom Christ died, we're apt to value them more. And, naturally, then we'd treat them a bit differently than we might were we to think they were nothing but a highly evolved monkey or nothing but "chemical scum" on the face of the planet.

Obviously, the human race is struggling with a form of schizophrenia regarding our identity. We'll either crawl or fly based on how we perceive ourselves.

Spiritual amnesia

My mother used to tell me that my brother Falcon and I had very different personalities. She remembered asking him, "Who do you think you are?" when he was just three or four years old. He'd always answer, "I'm Falcon Batchelor." A very confident and self-reliant individual, he never hesitated, never had any doubts. But when Mom asked me that same question, I would develop a brain cramp trying to find the answer. Falcon had a sense of self-awareness, but for me, it was a profound mystery. Not being raised with a biblical worldview, I didn't have satisfactory answers for the three big questions: Where did I come from? What am I doing here? Where am I going? These are the big questions everyone must resolve to have a life of purpose, direction, and security. It wasn't till I read the Bible and came to Christ that those questions were all fully answered for me.

It's easy to understand how someone with no biblical foundation could be so mystified about who they really are, but for a Christian to have that kind of identity crisis is a real tragedy. It's like being a disoriented scuba diver who can't tell which way is up and which is down. Divers who are disoriented swim in circles until they run out of air and drown. Like them, millions of people spend their entire lives not understanding the basic, defining issues: What is my past? What is my purpose for the present? And what is my goal for the future? That's why God laments, "My people have forgotten Me days without number" (Jeremiah 2:32).

Cases of complete amnesia are very rare, but they do happen. Someone may receive some kind of blunt trauma to the head, and his or her body may seem to be functioning normally, but the person doesn't know who he or she is anymore. I believe many Christians today are going through all the motions, but they're really bewildered—suffering from spiritual amnesia. They are unnerved into feeling insecure in their relationship with the Father, and so they fall into sin more easily. But it doesn't have to be this way—if they can discover who they really are.

---

1. Peter Gwynne, "The Secrets of the Human Cell," *Newsweek,* August 20, 1979, 48.

2. William Shakespeare, *Hamlet,* ed. Horace Howard Furness, 13th ed. (Philadelphia: J. B. Lippincott, 1905), act II, scene ii, lines 295–299.

3. Stephen Hawking, quoted in David Deutsch, *The Fabric of Reality* (New York: Penguin Books, 1998), 177, 178.

4. Reinhold Niebuhr, *Human Nature,* vol. 1, *The Nature and Destiny of Man: A Christian Interpretation* (Louisville, Ky.: Westminster John Knox Press, 1996), 1.

Chapter 2
A Prince or a Pauper?

He raises the poor out of the dust,
And lifts the needy out of the ash heap,
That He may seat him with princes—
With the princes of His people.

—Psalm 113:7, 8

Mark Twain's classic book *The Prince and the Pauper* tells the story of two boys who look virtually identical—Tom Canty, a pauper who lives with his abusive father in London, and Prince Edward, son of Henry VIII of England. Upon meeting each other, the boys agree to swap identities temporarily, so the poor boy learns to live as a prince, and the prince learns to live as a pauper.

Twain's book isn't the first to tell the story of a prince offering to trade places with a peasant. The Bible contains a similar story. As the firstborn son of King Saul, Jonathan was the crown prince of Israel. But Saul had become poisoned by pride and power and had turned away from God, so God sent Samuel the prophet to anoint a young shepherd named David to be the next king.

Soon after this David killed the giant Goliath. It was this famous battle that brought Jonathan and David together. Somehow, Jonathan knew of David's divine destiny. Instead of feeling threatened, he admired the young shepherd, and he did something remarkable—he relinquished his right to the throne. "Then Jonathan and David made a covenant, because he loved him as his own soul. And Jonathan took off the robe that was on him and gave it to David, with his armor, even to his sword and his bow and his belt" (1 Sam-

AMAZING FACTS

INTERNATIONAL

P.O. Box 909

Roseville, CA 95678-0909

Enroll online!

¡Inscríbete en línea!

uel 18:3, 4). "And he [Jonathan] said to him, . . . 'You shall be king over Israel' " (1 Samuel 23:17).

This story is a moving precursor of what Jesus does for every believer. He gives us His spiritual armor and His robe of righteousness and makes a covenant of love with us. He takes our poverty and offers us His palace. He gives us the throne that He deserves, and He takes the punishment that we deserve—death. Martin Luther used to say it this way, "Learn to know Christ and him crucified. Learn to sing to him, and say, 'Lord Jesus, you are my righteousness, I am your sin. You have taken upon yourself what is mine and given me what is yours. You became what you were not, so that I might become what I was not.' "[1]

Years ago the Muslims of Calcutta would offer a yearly sacrifice for the atonement of their sins. The sinner would lay his hands on the head of a lamb or a kid without spot or blemish and say, "For my head I give thine." Then he would touch various parts of the animal—the ears, the mouth, the eyes—and say, "For my ears, thy ears; for my mouth, thy mouth," and so forth. Finally, he would exclaim, "For my life, thy life," and as he pronounced these words, the cleric would plunge a knife into the lamb's heart and declare the supplicant absolved of his sins.

Christians don't receive their absolution and their new identity through the sacrifice of an animal but through the selfless sacrifice of Jesus. I can't improve on the wording found in the classic book *The Desire of Ages:* "Christ was treated as we deserve, that we might be treated as He deserves. He was condemned for our sins, in which He had no share, that we might be justified by His righteousness, in which we had no share. He suffered the death which was ours, that we might receive the life which was His. 'With His stripes we are healed.' "[2]

From prince to prison to prime minister

Joseph, one of the fathers of the nation of Israel, experienced the most radical change possible in outward circumstances yet still remembered who he was. This handsome young prince of a wealthy nomad calibrated his life by the promises that God made to his father Jacob, his grandfather Isaac, and his great-grandfather Abraham. Sold as a slave by his jealous brothers, Joseph went from prince to pauper overnight, but he didn't let bitterness or anger define who he was. Even though his circumstances changed frequently, he never let the changes affect his attitude toward God or his perception of God's thoughts toward him.

I love the story of Joseph because, in spite of the fact that his brothers resented his dreams, God had a big plan for his life. Joseph knew that from the beginning. He had dreams in which God told him he would be a leader. God said, "I have wonderful things in store for you. Others will bow down before you."

Jacob, Joseph's father, made a coat of many colors for him, indicating that Jacob intended to give him the privileges due the firstborn. Joseph's brothers deeply resented that and sold him into slavery. Although he was sold as a slave, he never considered himself to be one. He acted like a noble, and he continued to rise in rank and in power because of his humble but dignified self-image.

Then Joseph was falsely accused and thrown in prison. But he refused to consider himself as merely a prisoner. He still saw himself through the eyes of God. He knew that God had something great planned for his life, and he carried himself that way. Joseph never allowed his outward circumstances to define who he was. Even in the prison, he was promoted—because those who knew him there said, "He's not like a prisoner."

Finally, when the pharaoh needed someone to oversee the preparation for the coming famine, he said, "There's something different about Joseph. He seems to be a natural leader. I'll make him prime minister." Though Joseph had just come from prison, he bore himself with the dignity of a prince. He was able to do so because he always knew who he was in his heavenly Father's eyes.

Did you get that? You need to know who you are in your heavenly Father's eyes. You need to see yourself as God sees you. You need to value yourself as God values you, which can be estimated only in the light of the Cross.

Stunted faith

There's no place in the Bible where this principle of faith is revealed more dramatically than in the story of the twelve spies. (See Numbers 13 and 14.) As the children of Israel are camped on the borders of the Promised Land prior to entering it, Moses sends spies to explore the land of Canaan and bring back a report of what they might expect. (See Deuteronomy 1:22.) When the spies entered the Promised Land on their reconnaissance mission, their attitudes differed strikingly. Ten of them could see only the obstacles there—the massive walls of Jericho and the giant enemy soldiers. Two of the scouts, Joshua and Caleb, saw the country as a rich, beautiful land.

After forty days of surveying the Promise Land, the spies returned and delivered their report. Joshua and Caleb showed a colossal cluster of grapes they'd brought back to show the people, and they said, "We went to the land where you sent us. It truly flows with milk and honey, and this is its fruit" (Numbers 13:27). But the other ten spies countered, "Nevertheless the people who dwell in the land are strong; the cities are fortified and very large; moreover we saw the descendants of Anak [giants] there" (verse 28). In other words, two of the spies saw the roses, while the other ten saw only thorns.

Unfortunately, the nation believed the negative report and began to complain. They didn't have the faith to believe that the God who had delivered them from Egypt could—and would—bring them all the way into the Promised Land. And because of their lack of faith, they had to wander in the wilderness for forty years. Only two of that entire generation made it from Egypt to the Promised Land: Joshua and Caleb, who believed that God would do what He promised to do. These two faithful men didn't focus on the obstacles. They focused on God.

What happened to the ten negative spies? They died in the wilderness and never made it to the Promised Land. Why? Because they didn't believe they could go in. The point here should be obvious. If we believe that God can help us overcome the obstacles that sin raises, He will. Jesus said, "All things are possible to him who believes" (Mark 9:23). That's a promise—it's a promise that we can overcome the obstacles that face us.

Solomon said, "As [a person] thinks in his heart, so is he" (Proverbs 23:7). The Israelites were slaves in Egypt for so long that they started to think they had no other future, even though God kept trying to tell them they were destined to be a great people. "Ye shall be unto me a kingdom of priests, and an holy nation" (Exodus 19:6, KJV). More than once they began to hallucinate about how great things were back in Egypt and said they wanted to return there. That's the epitome of an identity crisis!

How could those people, whom God had chosen, not know who they were? God was in their very midst, yet they still suffered from an appalling case of spiritual amnesia. Like modern Christians who suffer from this same affliction, their troubles stemmed from carnal thinking. It was this crisis of self that kept causing them to stumble—so much so that many of them never made it to the land flowing with milk and honey. They took their eyes off the goal and saw only the obstacles.

Once the Israelites finally did realize their high calling, God urged them to repeat their history so they would never forget it. That's why when they were on the borders of the Promised Land, Moses commanded them, "Only take heed to yourself, and diligently keep yourself, lest you forget the things your eyes have seen, and lest they depart from your heart all the days of your life. And teach them to your children and your grandchildren" (Deuteronomy 4:9).

Back to David

I like the story of David. In part, I like it because David was the youngest son, a mere shepherd boy. Maybe he was shorter than his brothers. As a matter of fact, the Bible tells us that when Samuel the prophet was going to anoint one of the sons of Jesse to be the next king, he picked out the tallest one and said, "Surely he's the one."

Jesse had left David, his youngest son and probably the shortest one, out in the hills, taking care of the sheep. But David didn't see himself in terms of his size. When Goliath came marching out in front of all of the Israelites and mocked them and challenged them, David's brothers didn't feel so tall anymore. They didn't want to fight the giant. But David wasn't afraid. While everyone else saw this giant as more than nine feet tall, David saw him as only five feet fifty-six inches tall. He was a man of optimistic perspective! He didn't see himself as short either, so he didn't act as if he were because he knew who he was and what his own worth was in the eyes of the only One who really mattered—God.

You've heard the ongoing concerns about North Korea. People are worried about Kim Jong Il, the dictator of that country—a very volatile, insecure despot. Kim Jong Il wears five-inch-high platform shoes because he's so self-conscious about his size. Adolf Hitler was too. I worry about a leader who's so insecure about his vertical status.

But David didn't see himself as small. He remembered that God had chosen him—that he was anointed. And he figured that if God delivered him from the lion and God delivered him from the bear, He could deliver him from the giant. David saw himself as someone God could use. We need to see ourselves that way too.

In June 2002, the Bureau of Justice published a follow-up study of more than 272,000 prisoners who had been released in 1994.[3] The findings were very disturbing. The researchers found that 67.5 percent of all the released prisoners were rearrested for another crime within three years. Fifty-one percent were back in prison. The psychologists who evaluated these disturbing statistics surmise that many prisoners never learn to see themselves as free citizens, so they revert to their old behavior patterns. In contrast, the personnel of Chuck Colson's Prison Fellowship Ministries have demonstrated that graduates of their program—in which inmates are invited to accept Christ and to participate in Bible study—have a dramatically lower percentage of recidivism.

Did you catch that important point? Those who continue to view themselves as criminals continue to act like criminals. So, who do you think you are? It's important that you know this because you're going to act like the person you think you are.

To truly understand ourselves and who we are, we need to try to understand how God views us. We need to understand ourselves from a viewpoint outside of ourselves. We need to understand that God knows us and loves us anyway. We need to understand that He sees us from a perspective that isn't limited by what other people or even by what we ourselves think. The opinion that God, our Creator, has about us was best expressed at the cross. He loves us so much that He died to give us life.

---

1. Quoted in J. I. Packer, *Growing in Christ* (Wheaton, Ill.: Crossway Books, 1994).

2. Ellen G. White, *The Desire of Ages* (Mountain View, Calif.: Pacific Press® Publishing Association, 1940), 25.

3. Patrick A. Langan and David J. Levin, *Recidivism of Prisoners Released in 1994,* special report prepared for the U.S. Department of Justice (Washington, D.C.: U.S. Department of Justice, 2002), http://bjs.ojp.usdoj.gov/content/pub/pdf/rpr94.pdf.

Chapter 3
From Prison to Palace

One can indeed come out of prison to reign,
even though born poor in the kingdom.
—Ecclesiastes 4:14, NRSV

Nelson Mandela, South African activist, served twenty-seven years in prison because of his struggle against apartheid. He spent much of his incarceration languishing in a single cell on Robben Island. Yet on April 27, 1994, less than five years after his release, he was elected president of the country that had imprisoned him. Talk about an astounding change of status!

The Bible contains several inspiring examples of individuals who had their standing and position radically changed from captivity to royalty, from the prison to the palace. We'll start with the story of Joseph.

Pharaoh sent and called Joseph, and they brought him quickly out of the dungeon; and he shaved, changed his clothing, and came to Pharaoh. . . .

. . . And Pharaoh said to Joseph, "See, I have set you over all the land of Egypt." Then Pharaoh took his signet ring off his hand and put it on Joseph's hand; and he clothed him in garments of fine linen and put a gold chain around his neck. And he had him ride in the second chariot which he had; and they cried out before him, "Bow the knee!" So he set him over all the land of Egypt (Genesis 41:14, 41–43).

I can't help but wonder whether young Joseph saw himself as the prince of Egypt when he was nothing more than the custodian of a dungeon. Did David see himself as the future king of Israel while following the south end of northbound sheep across the hills of Bethlehem? Did young Esther see herself as the queen of Persia when she was a lowly orphan among the Jewish captives and doing common chores for her cousin Mordecai? And what about Daniel? When he entered Babylon, the capital of the empire, as a teenage captive, did he think he would someday become chief of staff for the king? We know that the seeds of greatness were in each of these young Bible heroes. But they could only germinate when watered by faith and virtue.

God has royal plans for every believing child. If we're faithful in the little duties, God will lift us up as He did Joseph, Esther, and Daniel. The apostle Paul confirmed this when he said that God "hath raised us up together, and made us sit together in heavenly places in Christ Jesus" (Ephesians 2:6, KJV).

What if, when the kings of Egypt and Persia summoned Joseph and Esther to leave their lowly positions and come to the palace, they had refused to come? Those monarchs would have considered Joseph's and Esther's spurning of their invitations as tremendous insults worthy of death. Yet many respond this way to Jesus, offering lame excuses when He invites them to live and reign with Him. They're like the ungrateful guests in Jesus' parable whom a wealthy man invited to a feast, but who "all with one accord began to make excuses" (Luke 14:18). In Jesus' parable, the host says, "None of those men who were invited shall taste my supper" (verse 24).

Those words of the host warn us to consider carefully

what we're turning down when we say No to Jesus. We've been invited to the marriage supper of the Lamb. "The Spirit and the bride say, 'Come!' And let him who hears say, 'Come!' And let him who thirsts come. Whoever desires, let him take the water of life freely" (Revelation 22:17). We've been invited to live and reign with Jesus. "If we endure, we shall also reign with Him" (2 Timothy 2:12). We should instantly, enthusiastically, and gratefully accept this incredible invitation of grace!

Second chance in the palace?

In contrast to those who were elevated from the prison to the palace, there are those who once enjoyed the status of being king but lost their exalted position through persistent disobedience. Like them, there are millions who served Jesus in their youth but have drifted away. Can they ever be restored to the palace after they have lost it through bad behavior and neglect? The last words in the book of Jeremiah tell a fascinating story that offers hope to people who have done this.

> Now it came to pass in the thirty-seventh year of the captivity of Jehoiachin king of Judah, in the twelfth month, on the twenty-fifth day of the month, that Evil-Merodach king of Babylon, in the first year of his reign, lifted up the head of Jehoiachin king of Judah and brought him out of prison. And he spoke kindly to him and gave him a more prominent seat than those of the kings who were with him in Babylon. So Jehoiachin changed from his prison garments, and he ate bread regularly before the king all the days of his life. And as for his provisions, there was a regu-

lar ration given him by the king of Babylon, a portion for each day until the day of his death, all the days of his life (Jeremiah 52:31–34).

Consider carefully for a moment these beautiful symbols of salvation. Evil-Merodach, son of Nebuchadnezzar, was a great and gracious king of kings. This benevolent monarch lifted Jehoiachin from prison and "spoke kindly to him." Similarly, Jesus speaks words of grace and kindness to us. Jehoiachin was given "a more prominent seat." We receive a new status to live and reign with our King, Jesus. Jehoiachin changes from his prison garments and is given royal robes, and Christ gives us a new robe of righteousness. And Jehoiachin eats royal bread the rest of his life—just as we depend on the Word of God as our spiritual food. As David said,

> You prepare a table before me in the presence of my
> enemies;
> You anoint my head with oil;
> My cup runs over.
> Surely goodness and mercy shall follow me
> All the days of my life;
> And I will dwell in the house of the LORD
> Forever (Psalm 23:5, 6).

King Manasseh was practically the epitome of wickedness. But when he was carried off to prison, he became truly repentant and prayed that God would forgive him and restore him to the palace. And God answered his humble prayer. "Then Manasseh knew that the LORD was God" (2 Chronicles 33:13). If God can forgive Manasseh, He can forgive anyone.

Bigger thinking

Jesus had been preaching from Peter's boat. When He finished His sermon, He told Peter to take the boat farther out on the lake and let down his fishing net. Peter said that he fished all night and caught nothing, but then he did what Jesus said anyway, and his net was filled with fish. Those fishermen had never had or even seen a catch like that one. Following a carpenter's advice about fishing had never paid off so well. Peter realized that he had witnessed a miracle, and he fell down at Jesus' feet, and said, "Lord, You'd better depart from me. I'm a sinful man. I have no right to be in Your presence."

Do you know what Jesus said in reply? "Don't be afraid. Follow Me and I will make you a fisher of men." He was implying, "You see yourself as a fisher of fish. You see yourself as just a failure. I see what you can be. You need to see yourself through what I can do with you." Jesus was saying, "You've been satisfied going after smelly fish. I want you to go after beings made in God's image. You need to raise the bar of who you are by following Me" (see Luke 5:1–10).

Follow Jesus. It will change your future. You are of immense value to Him. That's why He died for you.

When Jesus first saw Nathanael—whom He hadn't met before—coming towards Him, He said, "Truly this is an Israelite in whom there is no guile." Nathanael said, "Lord, how do You know me?" And Jesus said, "I saw you when you were under the fig tree."

Realizing that Jesus knew who he was, Nathanael fell down at His feet and said, "You are the Savior of Israel!" Jesus said, "Are you impressed because I saw you under the fig tree? You're going to see greater things than these." (See John 1.) In other words, Jesus was saying, "You're thinking too small. I've got big plans for you."

I think that one of the greatest challenges God is faced with when He calls humans to do His work is that we think too small. Jesus wants us to think with more faith, to believe that He can do great things through us if we believe. "All things are possible to him who believes" (Mark 9:23), isn't that right? It's a promise of the Lord.

You need to remember that God has a plan for your life. But you also need to remember that the devil has a plan for your life too. You get to choose which plan you follow. If you just live for yourself, you'll end up following the devil's plan. (Not a pretty picture!) But if you submit your life to the Lord and place your heart in His hands, you'll accomplish His plan for you. Jeremiah tells us the Lord's intention. "I know the thoughts that I think toward you, says the LORD, thoughts of peace and not of evil, to give you a future and a hope" (Jeremiah 29:11).

God says, "I have a future for you." It's a hope. You won't reach what you're hoping for without faith and without pursuing it. You need to do something to activate God's plan for your life. Why not tell Him right now you want to begin?

Chapter 4
A New Name

He who has an ear, let him hear what the Spirit says to the churches.
To him who overcomes I will give some of the hidden manna to eat.
And I will give him a white stone, and on the stone a new name
written which no one knows except him who receives it.

—Revelation 2:17

As the story goes, before the days of rigorous, computer-ized airport security, a man stopped at a bar in the Los Angeles airport to "relax" for a few minutes before catching his plane. Then, realizing he had lost track of time, he raced out of the bar and quickly asked directions to the departure gate for flights to Oakland. After hurrying through a maze of terminals, he handed his ticket to the gate clerk and scurried onto the plane just as it was about to depart. Then he stowed his briefcase, slumped into his seat, and drifted off to sleep.

When the weary traveler awoke and realized two hours had passed, he was puzzled. Why was his one-hour flight taking so long? He asked a flight attendant about it—and discovered to his horror that instead of flying to Oakland, California, he was on his way to Auckland, New Zealand! Because he'd slurred the words when he asked about the gate to the Oakland flight, the person he'd asked for directions thought he'd said Auckland. So that poor man had to endure a twenty-three-hour-long round-trip flight.

Most of us try to avoid the confusion produced by mis-pronounced names, but others with a unique sense of humor actually promote it. Perhaps you've heard of Lear Jets? Well, the Lear family named their daughter Shanda—Shanda Lear! And I had a friend named Jerry Mellow who named his son Marshall. Can you imagine growing up with the name *Marshall Mellow*? Can you imagine going through school and having your friends call you Marshmallow? I've told my sons that they should marry a girl named Mary Ann. Then her name would be Mary A. Batchelor!

Francis "Mickey" Featherstone was an Irish American mobster and a member of an organized crime gang from Hell's Kitchen in New York City. Following his arrest in 1986 for murder, the authorities offered him the opportunity to begin a new life with the federal Witness Protection Program if he'd serve as a witness for the government. That meant Mickey had to forsake his former friends and his old life. He agreed to do it, and today, somewhere in North America, he has a new name and he's living a new life.

God promises His redeemed, "You shall be called by a new name, which the mouth of the LORD will name" (Isaiah 62:2). God has given each of His children a new identity in Christ, His Witness Protection Program's best Agent, replacing the identities that became ours in the Garden of Eden when the devil tried to steal from us our identities as children of God. Christ paid top dollar for us—with His blood—to provide this new identity. The Bible says that we are not our own. We belong to God. "For ye are bought with a price: therefore glorify God in your body, and in your spirit, which are God's" (1 Corinthians 6:20, KJV).

New name, new rights

Many years ago in the little town of Woodleigh, England, Annie Grey grew up knowing that she would one day marry the boy who lived next door, William Coltart. And Will knew that someday he would marry Annie. But he decided he should have some financial security before settling down with a family, so off he went to work in Australia for a while.

When Annie didn't hear from him for several years, she concluded that his love for her had faded, and she reluctantly married a very rich merchant in town, Jonathon Tong. As you have probably guessed, soon after this, Will returned. Of course, he was heartbroken when he found that his Annie was wedded to another man. Nevertheless, he settled down in his hometown, resolving never to marry.

Several years later, Jonathon died; Will, still pining for Annie, felt that now he could propose to her. But when Jonathon's will was read, it stated clearly that Annie was to be cut off without a penny if she married Will. Obviously, Jonathon sensed that Will and Annie still cared for each other, and he didn't like that.

But Jonathon hadn't known that while Will was living in Australia, he had changed his name to *John Temple*. And after much debate, the English court decided that Annie could marry John Temple and still keep her inheritance, despite her jealous husband's attempt to disinherit her. Will's new name gave him the legal right to a loving relationship and a fabulous inheritance as well. But the new name had to come first.

When Abram was ninety-nine years old, God changed his name from *Abram*, which means "father is exalted," to *Abraham*, which means "father of a multitude." He was certainly not the father of a multitude when the Lord gave him the new name, but he grew into the name he had accepted by faith. Speaking of Abraham, Romans 4:17 says that he believed "even God, who quickeneth the dead, and . . ."—notice the rest of this very important verse—"calleth those things which be not as though they were" (KJV). God can declare something to exist that is not yet a reality, and it becomes real when He says it.

The name *Jacob* means "con artist, supplanter, trickster,

joker," and that was what he was like before he wrestled with God. So God said, "I'm giving you a new name, because you've been following the old label and I want you to change. I want you to live up to your new name." And He gave him the name *Israel,* "prince with God."

The same thing happens when we accept Jesus. We become new people in Him because we are now covered in His righteousness. The perfect life that Jesus lived now becomes ours by faith. It's accounted to us as if we ourselves had lived it. This is what is known in the Bible as "righteousness by faith" or "justification." And when we receive Jesus and begin following Him, He gives us new names—the names *Christian* and *saint.* "Now, therefore, you are no longer strangers and foreigners, but fellow citizens with the saints and members of the household of God" (Ephesians 2:19). The idea that we should dare to call ourselves saints seems pretty arrogant and delusional. But the Bible tells us that God calls believers *saints.* And when we accept the names He gives us, we change. God declares things to be that are not, and by faith they become real.

In a sense, Satan stole our identities way back in the Garden of Eden when our first parents succumbed to his wiles. In a sense, he stole from us who and what we were meant to be—beings made in the image of God; beings who were created for eternal life.

The good news of the gospel is that in Jesus, God came to earth as a man and lived a perfect life. Now He offers to restore to us our true identities—identities found in Him, the only sinless Being to ever live on this earth. And the gospel allows us to claim, by faith, His identity and His perfect life, which restores us to what we should have been all along.

As we meditate upon the life and love of Jesus, we

gradually become transformed into His image. We start out being like Him in faith, wearing our new name though it doesn't always fit. As time goes by, we grow into it, and it becomes our own. "We all, with unveiled face, beholding as in a mirror the glory of the Lord, are being transformed into the same image" (2 Corinthians 3:18).

So when we begin to follow the Lord, He gives us new names—*Christian* and *saint*. He then invites us to embrace those new names by faith and to represent them in our lives.

Name-dropping

Some people in Hollywood have tried to build their careers by name-dropping. They frequently refer to some famous producer or actor, freely using that person's name, as though they know him or her intimately, while in reality they may not know that person at all. Their hope is that they'll gain clout, prestige, or special access by association.

Believe it or not, some professed Christians have used the name of God in the same way. Acts 19:13–17 tells the story of the seven sons of Sceva, who decided to use the name of Christ to cast out demons. Apparently, these itinerate Jewish exorcists saw Paul's gifts and thought, *Hey, Paul's really good at this! Maybe we should adjust our means of casting out devils. We'll use the name Paul uses!* At their next opportunity, they told the demons, "We adjure you by Jesus whom Paul preacheth" (verse 13, KJV).

The Bible says, "The evil spirit answered and said, Jesus I know, and Paul I know; but who are ye? And the man in whom the evil spirit was leaped on them, and overcame them, and prevailed against them, so that they fled out of that house naked and wounded" (verses 15, 16, KJV). Those young Jewish exorcists tried name-dropping with the devil.

They knew the name of Jesus, and they even knew how to pronounce it. But they didn't know the Lord Himself, and unfortunately for them, the devils recognized this fact!

Paul's life was so godly and consistent and his preaching so bold that even the devils knew who he was and trembled at his faith. In the colossal conflict between good and evil that's going on now, who does the devil think you are? Are you living in a way that threatens him? You may be thinking, *I don't want to be on the devil's radar screen!* The alternative is to live a lukewarm, nominal, mediocre Christian life that is no threat to the enemy. Remember, Paul said, "All who desire to live godly in Christ Jesus will suffer persecution" (2 Timothy 3:12). And Jesus said, "He who is not with Me is against Me" (Luke 11:23).

Taking His name in vain

Adopting God's name when we don't have a real and personal knowledge of Him is part of the sin the third commandment addresses. "Thou shalt not take the name of the LORD thy God in vain; for the LORD will not hold him guiltless that taketh his name in vain" (Exodus 20:7, KJV). We often think of this commandment as condemning profanity, and it surely includes that, but that isn't the central issue. To take the name of the Lord in vain means to call yourself a Christian but then live like people who don't claim to serve God.

In the eighteenth century, a satirist named Georg Christoph Lichtenberg once told a pretty pointed parable: "Once the good man was dead, one wore his hat and another his sword as he had worn them, a third had himself barbered as he had, a fourth walked as he did, but the honest man that he was—nobody any longer wanted to be that."[1] That says a lot. If we profess the name of Jesus, how important that we live the life that Jesus modeled for us to live.

Who Do You Think You Are?

When I was driving in Northern California a few years ago, I picked up a hitchhiker who was walking down the road. He had long hair and a beard, and he was wearing a white linen robe tied around the waist with a piece of cloth. He was even barefoot. I thought to myself, *This person is taking the concept of following Jesus very literally.* However, as I talked with him, I found that he was mainly interested in encouraging people to smoke marijuana for enlightenment. He said almost nothing about modeling the life and teachings of Jesus.

Being a real Christian means more than changing one's clothes or even being baptized. It means more than having one's name entered in the church books or holding a high office in the church. It means more than giving bundles of money to worthy causes. It means more than writing great books about Jesus or preaching inspiring sermons about faith. A Christian is someone who is like Christ in character.

Author Tony Campolo tells about being mugged at gunpoint while he was walking down the street in some large city. During the robbery, the thief asked him what he did for a living. Campolo answered, "I'm a Baptist minister."

"Oh, you're a Baptist!" exclaimed the thief. "So am I!"

This criminal considered himself to be a Christian!

Campolo's story reminds me of a newspaper ad that read, "Lost—one dog. Brown, scruffy hair with several bald spots. Right leg broken due to auto accident. Half a tail. Right eye missing. Left ear bitten off in a dog fight. Answers to the name 'Lucky.' " Obviously, that unfortunate little dog was Lucky in name only. Some Christians are like that. When we become Christians, we take the name of Jesus. Sadly, some people merely become "nominal" Christians, which means they're Christians in name only. These people are taking the name of the Lord in vain.

Brand name

During a recent trip to China, our family was accosted by a street merchant who offered to sell us gold Rolex watches for twenty dollars. Seeing the dubious expression on my face, he opened his portable display case and showed me a sample. Admittedly, it looked like a Rolex watch and even had the Rolex name on the face. But I declined his offer because I knew the watch he showed me was really just painted gold and its inner workings had probably been made in Hong Kong. It takes more than a label to make a watch a genuine Rolex. And it takes more than a label to make a person a genuine Christian. The heart must be authentic.

It's true that we become justified Christians as soon as we come to Christ through faith. But sanctification always follows genuine justification. When we bring the Master our hearts, He replaces them with new hearts, and we then live different lives. The new name will be confirmed by a transformed heart. The apostle Paul said that though he spoke with the tongue of angels, had the gift of prophecy, had all knowledge, gave all his goods to the poor, and sacrificed his life, if he didn't have love in his heart, all the good deeds were essentially worthless (see 1 Corinthians 13:1–3).

It is said that Alexander the Great once had a soldier in his army who developed a bad reputation. When the fighting became severe, the young man would start to retreat while everyone around him fought on. Alexander summoned this soldier, whose name was also Alexander, and said, "I hear how you're behaving in battle. Young man, you need to change either your behavior or your name! I don't want the name *Alexander* to be associated with cowardice."

When you say you're a Christian, you have a responsibility to uplift the name of God in word and in deed. Jesus began the Lord's Prayer with the words, "Our Father which art in heaven, hallowed [holy] be thy name" (Matthew 6:9, KJV). If we take the name of the Lord in vain, we're making our Father's good name look bad.

Are you really you?

I heard about a woman who stepped into an elevator in New York and discovered that she was alone with the famous actor Robert Redford. As the elevator ascended, the woman, like many of us might, found herself repeatedly glancing at the movie star. Finally, she nervously asked, "Are you the real Robert Redford?" Redford responded, "Only when I'm alone."

So who is the real you?

Virtually everywhere you go these days there are cameras watching—in the stores, on the street, in cell phones, and on the satellites in the sky. It's no secret that people behave differently when they believe others are watching them. Jesus addressed this inclination we all have to court the praise of men. He said too many religious leaders like people to know about their giving, praying, and fasting. He warned, "Take heed that you do not do your charitable deeds before men, to be seen by them. Otherwise you have no reward from your Father in heaven" (Matthew 6:1).

In the end we need to ask who we want to impress—mortal humans or the God who offers us immortality? Of course, it's God who ultimately sees and records everything we say and do, including our motives. Obviously, to impress Him, our hearts must be transformed. All heaven is watching to find creatures here who are loyal to God and are living holy lives before Him. "Before him no creature is hidden, but all are naked and laid bare to the eyes of the one to whom we must render an account" (Hebrews 4:13, NRSV).

A New Name

The football Super Bowl draws more than one hundred million television viewers. Prices for advertising during the big game can cost up to three million dollars for thirty seconds—the highest prices advertisers ever pay. Why are they willing to pay so much? Because they know millions of people are watching.

You can imagine what care goes into preparing the advertisements that cost so much to broadcast. How careful would you be about your behavior if you knew that more than one hundred million people were watching you? But an audience much bigger than any Super Bowl audience *is* watching us! All of heaven is tuned into what is happening here on earth; not only God, which should be enough, but also "an innumerable company of angels" (Hebrews 12:22).

Jesus said, "Whoever confesses Me before men, him the Son of Man also will confess before the angels of God. But he who denies Me before men will be denied before the angels of God" (Luke 12:8, 9).

Solomon summed it up pretty well when he said,

Let us hear the conclusion of the whole matter:

Fear God and keep His commandments,
For this is man's all.
For God will bring every work into judgment,
Including every secret thing,
Whether good or evil (Ecclesiastes 12:13, 14).

Now is the time to choose who we really want to be and before whom we want to be real.

---

1. Georg Christoph Lichtenberg, *The Waste Books,* trans. R. J. Hollingdale (New York: New York Review of Books, 2000), 39.

Chapter 5
Visions of Grandeur

*If anyone thinks himself to be something,
when he is nothing, he deceives himself.*

—Galatians 6:3

While considering what it means to have a biblical perspective regarding who we are, we must remember we can easily err on either extreme, thinking too highly of ourselves or thinking too little of ourselves. A cow would never be comfortable trying to fly with the eagles or trying to dig with the gophers. It's happiest when it's munching grass in a green meadow. As we've been saying, many have too low an estimate of what we can become through Christ. Then of course there are those at the other end of the spectrum who have a delusionally proud perspective regarding who they are.

An extreme example would be Joshua Abraham Norton, or as he preferred to be called His Imperial Majesty Norton I. Norton immigrated to San Francisco from South Africa in 1849. After losing a fortune through some bad business deals, he became mentally unbalanced. In 1859, he began to boldly proclaim himself the emperor of the United States. He ordered that the United States Congress be dissolved by force, and he issued decrees calling for a bridge to be built across San Francisco Bay. (The construction of the San Francisco-Oakland Bay Bridge eventually fulfilled this dictate!)

Many people found it entertaining to play along with Norton's delusion. Although a pauper, he ate in San Francisco's best restaurants for free. And even though he was generally considered insane or at least highly eccentric, San Francisco's newspapers published all his "state proclamations." The citizens of San Francisco—and the world at large—celebrated his peculiar presence, his humor, and his deeds.

While Norton's visions of grandeur may have been a humorous oddity, God has a sober perspective on those who have an inflated view of their spiritual status. We must guard against falling into the smug, arrogant, Laodicean problems of the last-day church that thinks it is far better off than it really is. Revelation 3:17 warns, "You say, 'I am rich, have become wealthy, and have need of nothing'—and do not know that you are wretched, miserable, poor, blind, and naked." Isn't Jesus saying here, "You don't know who you really are"? The last-day church is wretched and poor, but its members think they are superior and rich. We desperately need to grasp who we really are and what our true condition is. Otherwise we are delusional.

We're better off thinking a little less of ourselves than exalting ourselves too highly in our own eyes. Someone has said that we're never more like the devil than when we're proud. Jesus gave an example: "When you are invited [to a wedding]," He said, "go and sit down in the lowest place, so that when he who invited you comes he may say to you, 'Friend, go up higher.' Then you will have glory in the presence of those who sit at the table with you. For whoever exalts himself will be humbled, and he who humbles himself will be exalted" (Luke 14:10, 11). And the apostle Paul tells us, "I say, through the grace given to me, to everyone who is among you, not to think of himself more highly than he ought to think, but to think soberly, as God has dealt to each one a measure of faith" (Romans 12:3).

So we shouldn't think unrealistically well of ourselves,

but at the same time it's just as problematic when we put on false humility. Some people think it's a Christian virtue to deny who they really are. That would be like Tiger Woods saying, "Well, I don't really know much about golf. I'm not that good." Would that be honest? Is that being humble, or is that simply rank lying?

Statements like that are just plain untruthful. That's not humility. We shouldn't think less of ourselves than is the case, nor should we think too highly of ourselves. So, ask God to give you a humble yet realistic and balanced perspective of what you can do and who you are. Then make sure to give Him the glory for all your gifts and natural abilities.

Regarding the matter of who we are in the Lord, I think we are more likely to think too small than too big. Our motivation is important—we want to know who we are in God for His glory. We shouldn't look to the world to find out who we are, and we shouldn't be ashamed of who we are. Too often we're too preoccupied with being popular in the world, but it's more important that we're popular in heaven. That's where we're ultimately going to be judged. Jeremiah 45:5 commands, "Do you seek great things for yourself? Do not seek them." Is it OK to seek great things? Yes, but the key is not "for yourself"! Seek great things for God, and He will show you who you are.

Overconfident

As a young man seeking to exterminate the Christian religion, Saul, who later became the apostle Paul, felt fairly confident that he knew who he was. He truly believed that he was serving the Lord and that God's blessing attended his efforts—that is until Jesus confronted him with the truth.

On the road to Damascus, Saul suddenly realized he wasn't working for God but for the devil. He definitely wasn't who he thought he was (Acts 9).

Peter thought he knew himself, so when Jesus said that all the disciples would forsake Him that night, he confidently boasted, "Even if all are made to stumble because of You, I will never be made to stumble." Jesus said to him, "Assuredly, I say to you that this night, before the rooster crows, you will deny Me three times." But Peter disagreed. "Even if I have to die with You, I will not deny You!" (Matthew 26:33–35). Peter was probably sincere, but he grossly overestimated his courage. Before twenty-four hours had passed, he had denied Jesus three times.

King Hezekiah was told by the prophet Isaiah that he was terminally ill. The good king turned his face to the wall and cried and prayed and cited his virtues to God: "Remember now, O Lord, I pray, how I have walked before You in truth and with a loyal heart, and have done what was good in Your sight" (2 Kings 20:3). He had a lofty estimate of his own dedication.

God healed Hezekiah, and then He allowed him to be tested. When ambassadors came from Babylon to learn about the God who had just healed his terminal disease, Hezekiah flaunted his wealth and power in front of them and never mentioned God at all. The ambassadors took note of his treasure, and eventually, the king of Babylon returned to ransack and loot Jerusalem.

But there's good news in all these biblical passages. God gave Peter, Paul, and Hezekiah fresh revelations of who they were. The healthy humiliation they experienced brought them into a saving relationship with Him.

Overconfidence boils down to simple pride. "The evil that led to Peter's fall and that shut out the Pharisee from communion with God is proving the ruin of thousands today. There is nothing so offensive to God or so dangerous to the human soul as pride and self-sufficiency. Of all sins it is the most hopeless, the most incurable."[1]

The placebo effect

As we explore the importance of understanding who we are, we need to consider the power of faith. As I have mentioned, people's concepts of who they are generally influence how they behave. In other words, our concepts of who we are will define what we become. Some people are inclined to think, *Oh, I'm just a failure.* If we think that often enough, we *will* be failures. We're affected by our own words. Many times after Jesus healed people, He told them, "Go your way. Your faith has made you well" (Luke 17:19; see also Mark 10:52). He didn't say, "My faith"; He said, "Your faith." We just noted that Paul wrote, "God has dealt to each one a measure of faith" (Romans 12:3). And very often Jesus said, "According to your faith let it be to you" (Matthew 9:29). Scripture also says, "As [a person] thinketh in his heart, so is he" (Proverbs 23:7, KJV).

Since we generally grow into what we think we are, we each need to ask ourselves, *Do I think I'm a child of the king, a child of the devil, or something in-between? Do I think I'm victorious or defeated? Do I believe I'm destined to be a slave or a prince?* "According to your faith let it be to you."

I want you to explore who you are in Bible terms. That's how you can get an accurate picture of who you are to God, the One who created you and who knows you better than anyone else does.

You've probably heard of the placebo effect. It's an illustration of the fact that what we think has a powerful effect on our bodies. Here's something amazing that was in the *New York Times Magazine* in 2000—a series of studies about the placebo effect.

> Doctors in one study successfully eliminated warts by painting them with a brightly colored, inert dye and promising patients the warts would be gone when the color wore off. And it worked. In a study of asthmatics, researchers found that they could produce dilation of the airways by simply telling people they were inhaling a bronchiodilator, even when they weren't. Patients suffering pain after wisdom-tooth extraction got just as much relief from a fake application of ultrasound as from a real one, so long as both patient and therapist thought the machine was on. Fifty-two percent of the colitis patients treated with placebo in 11 different trials reported feeling better— and 50 percent of the inflamed intestines actually looked better when assessed with a sigmoidoscope.[2]

There are also many cases in which people get sick because they think they're sick. For example, some people have received the wrong lab report, and the doctor says, "Evidently you've got this virus, and you're very ill." Well, they mistakenly got the report of someone else's blood work, but they start feeling sick right away. And then they get a phone call a few weeks later and someone tells them, "We're so sorry. That wasn't your report. You're actually in perfect health." But by now they're in bed and they have a fever and they're feeling lousy because they believe they're sick. Are you beginning to get a picture of how what you think can influence who you are physically?

Many people think, *Oh, I doubt I'll ever enter the Promised Land.* Like those ten faithless spies, they come to the borders of Canaan and they're ready to cross over, but then they look at the obstacles and say, "I don't see how I can ever make it. The enemy is going to conquer me. I'll die in the wilderness." You know what happened to those negative messengers? They and everybody who believed them died in the wilderness just as they'd feared they would. They didn't see themselves in the Promised Land, and so they didn't make it. "According to your faith let it be to you."

But Joshua and Caleb said, "We can make it! Let's go right now." And even though they had to wander a while with the faithless, they made it, didn't they? "According to your faith let it be to you."

There's a very dangerous teaching that circulates among many professed Christians: God forgives our sin. We like that teaching. We all want the forgiveness. Of course, it's true. The problem is that people go on to say that God doesn't really expect us to get victory over sin, that we're not saved *from* our sin. But before Jesus' birth, the angel told Joseph, "You shall call His name JESUS, for He will save His people *from* their sins" (Matthew 1:21; emphasis added). But now people say that God saves us *in* our sin. That doctrine is becoming popular because everyone says, "I don't see how I could ever be an overcomer. I don't see how God could ever change me." If you start thinking that way, well, that's the way it's going to be. But if you believe that God can give you the victory, that the God you serve is bigger than the devil, and that you can be a new creature and all things can be made new, then it will be. It is so important that we understand and accept by faith what Christ did to free us.

So often we're tempted to believe that the devil is still in charge of our lives. We forget that, at the cross, Jesus defeated him. Now, "sin shall not have dominion over you" (Romans 6:14). We need to say and believe that through Christ, all things are possible—that we can do all things through Him (Philippians 4:13). He lives in us. We don't need to submit as slaves to the devil any longer. If you truly believe that, it will be unto you according to your faith. This doesn't mean that you won't be tempted or that Satan will never again try to assert his old dominance. Struggles continue throughout the Christian life, but the biggest struggle is for faith. However, Scripture says you aren't the old you. You're a new person. Old things have passed away. All things are made new (see 2 Corinthians 5:17).

I know of a pastor who would address backslidden church members as though they were already becoming active Christians again. The pastor would boldly ask these prodigals to visit a lonely neighbor who needed encouragement and prayer. The backslidden members would think, *Me? I should pray for them? I've been away so long!* Yet often they sheepishly start living out the pastor's expectations, and their connection with God becomes real again.

The same thing happens with bad habits such as smoking. I've kicked the habit and have helped others do it, too, and I know that people who are in the process of quitting shouldn't say, "I'm trying to quit smoking." No. Instead, they should make a decision and then announce it to everyone: "I've quit smoking." There's a big difference; quitters need to see themselves as free from smoking. They need to change their pictures of themselves. As I noted earlier in chapter 4, "God . . . calls those things which be not as though they were" (Romans 4:17, KJV).

If you forever see yourself as morally fallen and a captive of the devil, you'll be spiritually paralyzed. You've got to see yourself as free. Jesus promised, "If the Son therefore shall make you free, ye shall be free indeed" (John 8:36, KJV). Are you *trying* to be free, or has Jesus already made you free? See the difference? God tells us we are saints! Paul told the believers in Colossae that the Father has "qualified us to be partakers of the inheritance of the saints in light" and has "delivered us from the power of darkness" (Colossians 1:12, 13). Will God deliver us sometime in the future, or has He already delivered us? Paul says the latter. When you believe it by faith, it becomes real. Jesus said, "According to your faith let it be to you" (Matthew 9:29).

Augustine, a famous theologian of the early Christian church, admitted that before he was converted, he lived a very profane and immoral life. Sometime after his radical new birth, he was walking down a street in Milan, Italy, and one of his old girlfriends saw him. She was amazed that he looked right at her but kept going without even a nod of recognition. She chased him down the street, calling out, "Augustine, it is I! It is I!" He turned toward her and said, "But it is no longer I." This is the essence of the true righteousness by faith. You become righteous when you believe God's promises. Through the prophet Ezekiel, God made a promise to those who would choose to be His people: "I will put a new spirit within them, and take the stony heart out of their flesh, and give them a heart of flesh, that they may walk in My statutes and keep My judgments and do them; and they shall be My people, and I will be their God" (Ezekiel 11:19, 20).

So, who do you think you are? All things are new when you are in Christ. You're new, too, if you are in Christ, and it's wonderful when you start to envision it, embrace it, and make it real for your life. Don't let the world define who you are. Don't let the devil define who you are. Let God's Word define who you are. Who has Jesus declared you to be? He says you're His child. He says He's called you and me to be a nation of kings and priests.

Children of a king

I remember reading, long ago, a story from history. Some European dynasty was embroiled in a revolution—a coup of some sort, and the upper echelons of society were being decimated by the revolutionaries. A faithful servant of the imperial family was in charge of getting the royal children safely out of the country. Disguised and fleeing under cover of darkness, they left the castle and the city and found refuge somewhere deep in the woods a long way away from the violence.

The servant eventually brought the children to the border of a friendly country where they would be safe, though bereft of their former wealth and titles. They would, more than likely, be reduced to living a common life of obscurity in their new land, but they *would* live. Before departing, the servant gave them final instructions from their parents, who by now were dead. "The one thing," said the servant, "that your parents wanted you to remember more than anything else was who you really are. No matter your circumstances, no matter your struggles or your fears, never forget that you are children of a king and conduct yourselves as such."

Who do you think you are? You're the children of a King— and not just any king, but the King of the universe! Where do you think you belong? On the winning team! You don't need to continue to suffer spiritual amnesia. You don't need to continue in the depths of an identity crisis. "Behold what manner of love the Father has bestowed on us, that we should be called children of God!" (1 John 3:1). Salvation is all about getting a new identity. The more we remember who we are in God—the children of a King—the more willing we'll be to shake off our allegiance to the devil. We'll cease to be slaves of the archfiend, and we'll become servants of the Lord.

Jesus has declared that He has adopted us and invited us to be a nation of kings and priests (Revelation 1:5, 6). So, we need to conduct ourselves like royalty. He's told us we're soldiers in His army, and He's given us a rank and a great mission. "You are a holy people to the LORD your God; the LORD your God has chosen you to be a people for Himself, a special treasure above all the peoples on the face of the earth" (Deuteronomy 7:6). God has called us to be His special treasure. Jesus has promoted us. He's handed us victory over the devil. But all of this won't do us any good until we embrace it with our gray matter. So, who do you think you are?

Being rich, but living poor

Who do you think you are? Your concept of yourself will make all the difference in the world as to what kind of life you live. My heart breaks when I see talented young people living beneath their inheritance. God has such big plans for their lives, but they're not living them. God could do so much through them if they would only see themselves differently. So often the young people of today are allowing mass media to define who they are, and they end up falling into a vortex of fashion, rock music idols, and drugs. They're thinking they're going to find happiness and purpose in fame and fortune and having all the toys, and they don't see who they are in God. They forget that we have treasure in heaven.

When Ned Green broke his leg during the late 1800s, his mother, Hetty, did her best to treat it herself, thinking the hospitals in New York City were far too expensive. But after a few days, Ned's leg became infected. Hetty sadly shook her head. She knew only a doctor could help him at that point.

Knowing how much the private hospitals charged for patient care, Hetty loaded her fever-racked son into an old carriage and began searching from one end of Manhattan to the other for a free clinic where the poor were treated for little or no money. When Hetty finally found one, the doctor made a brief examination of the boy's swollen leg and shook his head. "I'm sorry, ma'am," he said. "The infection has spread so far that all I can do now is remove his leg. If only you had brought him in sooner." Ned cried and pleaded, "No, please don't take off my leg." But the doctor had no choice. The gangrenous leg had to be amputated.

The frustrated physician must have thought, *This unfortunate boy will live out the rest of his life as an invalid because this poor woman couldn't afford basic medical attention.* He didn't know that "Hetty"—Henrietta Howland Green— was far from poor. At the time of her son's injury, she was the world's richest woman—and probably the world's stingiest too. When she died, she was worth between 1.9 and 3.8 billion dollars in today's money!

Also known as the Witch of Wall Street, Hetty was legendary for her eccentric penny-pinching. Not only was she willing to let her son lose his leg rather then pay for medical treatments, she never turned on the heat nor used hot water. She wore one old black dress and bought broken cookies in bulk because they were cheaper. She would travel thousands of miles to collect a debt of a few hundred dollars. One tale claims that she spent a whole night looking for a lost two-cent postage stamp! As penurious as she was, I still have to wonder how somebody with so much money could neglect the basic needs of her child. What Jesus said was certainly true of Hetty: "Where your treasure is, there your heart will be also" (Matthew 6:21).

When we're adopted into the family of God, we gain a Father who owns the biggest bankbook in the universe. It's filled with grace. Yet we're so slow to make a withdrawal—even though the Word of God promises, "My God shall supply all your need according to His riches in glory by Christ Jesus" (Philippians 4:19).

So how do we make a withdrawal? We simply have to—through faith and by prayer—ask! "What man is there among you who, if his son asks for bread, will give him a stone? Or if he asks for a fish, will he give him a serpent? If you then, being evil, know how to give good gifts to your children, how much more will your Father who is in heaven give good things to those who ask Him!" (Matthew 7:9–11).

God is much more willing to answer our prayers than we are to even pray them. And He's more willing to satisfy our needs than earthly parents are to feed their hungry children. Jesus said, "Hitherto have ye asked nothing in my name: ask, and ye shall receive, that your joy may be full" (John 16:24, KJV).

I'll close this chapter with a quotation that I love, "Why should the sons and daughters of God be reluctant to pray, when prayer is the key in the hand of faith to unlock heaven's storehouse, where are treasured the boundless resources of Omnipotence?"[3]

1. Ellen G. White, *Christ's Object Lessons* (Mountain View, Calif.: Pacific Press®, 1941), 154.

2. Margaret Talbot, "The Placebo Prescription," *New York Times Magazine,* January 9, 2000.

3. Ellen G. White, *Steps to Christ* (Washington, D.C.: Review and Herald®, 1956), 94, 95.

Chapter 6
Whose Do You Think You Are?

Thus said the LORD of hosts . . . : Truly, one who
touches you touches the apple of my eye.

—Zechariah 2:8, NRSV

For their honeymoon, an American couple went on an adventurous vacation in the outback of Australia. One day, they drove their rented Jeep into a small, remote outback town. The husband wanted to go to a ranch on the outskirts of the town, where the Australian technique for breaking wild horses was being demonstrated. His wife, an attractive young woman, was more interested in purchasing a few of the local curios made by Aborigines to take home as gifts for her friends and family. So the husband dropped her off at the porch of the only store in town, which also served as a gift shop in addition to being a grocery store and a hardware store.

The wife spent about forty minutes casually selecting gifts, and then it was time for the shop to close for the day, so she went to the front porch to wait for her groom. About the same time a gaggle of five men stumbled out of the pub next door, obviously inebriated. Seeing the pretty young woman who was waiting on the porch of the store, they joined her there. Then, with a bravado born of beer, a couple of the men began to make lewd suggestions to the woman. At first she ignored them, silently looking up the road with her arms folded over her bag of gifts. But the men, still nursing their beers, continued to become more bold and obnoxious with each sip. "Aw, come on, deary," one of them said, "just give us all a little kiss and we'll leave you alone."

The woman responded, "You don't know who you're insulting."

Surprised by her response, one of the offenders slurred, "My, you're awfully brave, considering there's only one of you and five of us."

The woman confidently replied, "If you're smart, you'll leave me alone"—which only made the men laugh.

But then the groom came zipping around the corner in the Jeep. As he pulled up to the platform where his bride was waiting, he could see that she was upset, and it was obvious that her discomfort had something to do with the drunken men behind her. The groom stepped out of the Jeep, and it rose up a full six inches on squeaking springs. He was a professional wrestler—six feet eight inches tall and 290 pounds of hard muscle. He walked up to the porch with his biceps rippling and asked the drunks, "Is there a problem, gentlemen?"

The stunned men stuttered, "No problem here, mate. None at all."

As the woman climbed into the Jeep, proud of her powerful husband, she couldn't resist casting a triumphant look at the suddenly sobered men. With her husband there, she felt safe.

We must never forget whose we are. We must never forget that as the church, we are the bride of Christ, we are the apple of His eye—the only object on earth upon which He bestows His supreme regard. Using the metaphor of marriage, the apostle Paul tells us that Christ loved the church so much that He "gave Himself for her" (Ephesians 5:25).

As we await the return of our Groom, this wicked world may abuse us. After all, we've been warned that "all who desire to live godly in Christ Jesus will suffer persecution" (2 Timothy 3:12).

But now, thus says the LORD, who created you, O Jacob,
And He who formed you, O Israel:
"Fear not, for I have redeemed you;
I have called you by your name;
You are Mine" (Isaiah 43:1).

When you are abused for your faith, remember to whom you belong.

The Bible teaches that when Jesus comes, He will rescue and vindicate His persecuted bride. And Paul said that God will "repay with tribulation those who trouble you, and to give you who are troubled rest with us when the Lord Jesus is revealed from heaven with His mighty angels, in flaming fire taking vengeance on those who do not know God, and on those who do not obey the gospel of our Lord Jesus Christ" (2 Thessalonians 1:6–8). "As the bridegroom rejoices over the bride, so shall your God rejoice over you" (Isaiah 62:5).

Never forget whose you are, and that you plus God always constitute a majority.

Identity by adoption

When Jesus was baptized, God the Father's voice boomed down from heaven: "This is My beloved Son, in whom I am well pleased" (Matthew 3:17). Jesus was God's Son in a sense that will never be true of us. But the Father wants to make us part of His family. He wants to adopt us. "He chose us in Him before the foundation of the world, that we should be holy and without blame before Him in love, having predestined us to adoption as sons by Jesus Christ to Himself" (Ephesians 1:4, 5).

One day two boys presented themselves to a Sunday School teacher and asked to join her class. In the process of registering them, she asked their ages and birthdays. The bolder of the two said, "We're both seven. My birthday is April 8, 1976, and my brother's is April 20, 1976."

"But that's impossible!" answered the teacher.

"No, it's not," answered the quieter brother. "One of us is adopted."

Before the teacher could catch herself, she asked, "Which one?"

The boys looked at each other and smiled, and the bolder one said, "We asked Dad a while ago, but he just said he loved us both, and he couldn't remember anymore which one was adopted."

When we're born into the family of God, He looks upon us as completely and fully His.

Mistaken identity

A novelist couldn't have written a stranger story. On April 26, 2006, a tractor trailer, speeding down Interstate 69 near Marion, Indiana, struck a Taylor University van, killing four students and one school employee. A fifth student, a young woman identified as Laura Van Ryn, survived. But she was severely injured and in a coma.

The Van Ryn family spent weeks by Laura's side, encouraging her slow, but steady recovery. Then one day in a therapy session as she was gaining semiconsciousness, she wrote that her name was Whitney. When she was asked again what her name was, she said faintly, "I'm Whitney." Then began the process of getting a positive identification, which confirmed that the girl the Van Ryn family had been caring for wasn't Laura; she was Whitney Cerak, an acquaintance of Laura's who'd been in the van too.

How had the identities of the two young women been

switched? Apparently, in the chaos after the crash, the paramedics placed the wrong purses and IDs with the girls. When the Cerak family was told their daughter had died in the collision, they didn't want their last memory of her to be what she looked like in the morgue, so they didn't view the body.

The problem was compounded because these two young women were about the same size and had the same color hair and similar complexions. And with the bruises and swelling caused by the crash, even their own parents found it hard to recognize them.

How tragic for the Van Ryn family to discover that the patient they had prayed for and cared for during the past five weeks wasn't their Laura—that their daughter had been buried a month earlier in a mismarked grave. Conversely, of course, the Cerak family must have felt that their Whitney, for whom they had grieved and whom they had laid to rest, had in effect been resurrected. Talk about mistaken identity!

Fortunately, God knows those who are His. If we serve Him in this life and die before Jesus returns, He'll raise us up in a genuine resurrection, and we'll spend eternity with Him. And there'll be no mistaking who we are. We'll know fully and even as we have been fully known (see 1 Corinthians 13:12).

Bat: bird or beast?

Knowing whose you are requires loyalty to God's people. If you have accepted Jesus and committed your life to Him, you can't serve someone else too. No one can serve two masters (see Luke 16:13).

Aesop told a fable about a war between the beasts and the birds. In his story, the bat tried to belong to both parties. When the birds were victorious, he would fly around, telling everyone that he was a bird. And when the beasts won a battle, he would walk around with them, assuring them that he was a beast. But soon his hypocrisy was discovered, and both the beasts and the birds rejected him. That's why, so the fable concludes, ever after that, he's had to hide himself in caves and come out only at night.

We also face the temptation to waffle back and forth between our identities. If we are the children of God and made in His image, we should consistently conduct ourselves as such. But many times when we're under pressure from the world around us, we'll resume the old carnal personality and forget who we really are. Paul reminds us "that our old man was crucified with [Jesus], that the body of sin might be done away with, that we should no longer be slaves of sin" (Romans 6:6). We must be prepared at all times to resist the inclinations of our old natures. Again, Paul tells us to "put off, concerning your former conduct, the old man which grows corrupt according to the deceitful lusts, and be renewed in the spirit of your mind, and that you put on the new man which was created according to God, in true righteousness and holiness" (Ephesians 4:22–24).

No one can serve two masters. Christians who try to live two lives won't have either the respect of the world or the peace of God. Jesus warned strongly against becoming spiritual hypocrites. He condemned the religious charlatans who would pray, fast, and give charity solely for the sake of their image, while in reality they had no genuine love for God or humanity.

A chicken or an eagle?

Many go through life with a faulty concept of faith because they have never seen the genuine item lived out before them. Surrounded from birth by nominal Christians and fed on faithless theology, they have never even considered what great things God actually has in store for genuine believers.

An old story has it that a naturalist visiting a farm was surprised to see an eagle in the farmer's chicken coop, pecking at grain and waddling awkwardly in circles. Puzzled, he asked, "Why in the world is that eagle living with those chickens?"

"Well," answered the farmer, "I found an abandoned eagle's egg one day out on the bluffs. I put it in the coop, and a chicken decided to sit on it. Amazingly, the egg hatched, and the chickens adopted the eaglet as if it were just an ugly chick. With a little help from me, they raised the creature. That bird doesn't know any better. It thinks it's a chicken."

"Doesn't it ever try to fly out of there?" asked the naturalist, noticing that the bird never lifted its gaze.

"No," said the farmer. "I doubt it even knows what it means to fly."

The naturalist asked permission to conduct a few experiments with the eagle, and the farmer agreed. First, the naturalist perched the eagle on a fence and then pushed it off, saying, "Fly!" But the noble bird just fell to the ground and started pecking.

Next, the naturalist carried the eagle to the top of a hayloft and launched it into the air from there. But the frightened bird merely shrieked and fluttered ingloriously down to the barnyard, where it resumed its strutting on the ground.

Finally, the naturalist took the docile eagle away from the environment to which it had grown accustomed, and took it to the highest butte in the county. After a grueling climb to the hillcrest, with the bird tucked under his arm, the naturalist peered over the edge, and then spoke gently. "Friend," he said, "you were born to soar. It's better that you die here on the rocks than live the rest of your life being a chicken. That's not what you are."

Suddenly, the confused bird glimpsed another eagle soaring on the air currents high above the bluff. It cocked its head and stared intently, and it seemed that a new yearning was kindled within it. Just then the naturalist threw the majestic bird over the edge of the bluff, crying out, "Fly! Fly! Fly!"

At first the baffled bird just tumbled and struggled, spiraling toward the rocks below. But then, instinctively, it opened its seven-foot span of wings and began to flap them. It flew clumsily at first, but soon it was gliding gracefully, rising up into the blue sky. With a mighty screech, it began climbing ever higher, circling on unseen thermals. Soon, the mighty eagle disappeared into the glare of the morning sun.

We were created in the image of God. He meant us to soar. He wants us to reach for the heavens. But the devil has many of us content to scratch around on the ground, living low. How sad! So I ask you again, Who do you think you are? "According to your faith let it be to you" (Matthew 9:29).

God tells you and me that He has called us to be a nation of kings and priests. You're alive today because God wants you to know that He has a big plan for your life. Don't let the devil define who you are. You need to believe that God has declared you to be victorious. You need to start being the person He has said you are.

Satan stole your true identity; Christ has won it back for you. Claim what's rightfully yours.

You wouldn't let a human thief get away with stealing your identity, would you? Of course not. Then why let Satan? You don't have to. You can go to Jesus, who will give it back to you—and then some.

Chapter 7
You Are What You Wear!

Then He . . . spoke to those who stood before Him, saying, "Take away the filthy garments from him." And to him He said, "See, I have removed your iniquity from you, and I will clothe you with rich robes." And I said, "Let them put a clean turban on his head." So they put a clean turban on his head, and they put the clothes on him. And the Angel of the LORD stood by.
—Zechariah 3:4, 5

Human beings differ from every other creature in regards to clothing. All of the other creatures in God's kingdom were born with their clothes on, so to speak. The covering they need grows from the inside out, and some animals even shed their old clothes periodically and "put on" new ones. Human beings are the only creatures whose clothes must come entirely from the outside.

In the extreme temperatures and vacuum of interplanetary space, astronauts need special clothing in order to survive. Their pressurized space suits supply them with oxygen, keep their bodies at controlled temperatures, remove moisture from the air around them, and monitor their blood pressure and heart rhythms. When Neil Armstrong went on the *Apollo 11* mission that sealed his place in history as the first man to walk on the moon, his suit was specially designed to provide a life-sustaining environment during periods of extra vehicular activity or unpressurized spacecraft operation. The custom-fitted space suit was designed to be worn with relative comfort for up to 115 hours outside the spacecraft or for fourteen days in an unpressurized mode.[1]

Astronauts must put an enormous amount of trust in their spacesuits. One said it was eerie to realize that while he was outside the space capsule, there was just one-quarter of an inch of rubber between him and eternity. Now that's some important clothing!

It's also true that in the Christian life, we need to make sure we choose our garments carefully if we want to have an out-of-this-world experience!

On February 1, 2004, during the halftime show of Super Bowl XXXVIII and before a live audience of millions, Justin Timberlake tore away a piece of Janet Jackson's costume, baring her right breast. When people responded with outrage and the Federal Communications Commission threatened to lay a hefty fine on the network for the incident, Timberlake tried to blame the incident on an unintentional "wardrobe malfunction"—a phrase that has taken on a life of its own. It is now defined as "an accidental or supposedly accidental failure of clothing to cover parts of the body intended to be covered."[2] Journalist Eric Alterman described the Super Bowl incident as "the most famous 'wardrobe malfunction' since Lady Godiva."[3]

The Bible tells us that artificial clothing was first introduced after Adam and Eve ate the forbidden fruit in the Garden of Eden. Until that time, our first parents were likely clothed with garments or robes of light (see Mark 9:3). Scripture says that after they sinned, they had a big-time wardrobe malfunction: "The eyes of them both were opened, and they knew that they were naked; and they sewed fig leaves together, and made themselves aprons" (Genesis 3:7, KJV).

Adam and Eve had never witnessed death, so they probably thought the fig leaves would work just fine as a permanent cover-up for their shame. However, when the leaves began to shrivel, Adam and Eve experienced another wardrobe malfunction. God told the wayward couple that their skimpy fig-leaf "coverings" weren't adequate. He also explained that in order for them to be properly clothed, other creatures would have to be sacrificed. Innocent lambs would need to die to cover their nakedness, and their deaths would foreshadow the coming of God's Son Jesus, the Lamb of God, and His death to cover their sin. The Bible says that then God made garments of skin for Adam and Eve, clothing them (see Genesis 3:21).

Dress for success

John T. Molloy, author of *Dress for Success,* wanted to see how people respond to another person's appearance, so, during high traffic times, he panhandled for money at the Port Authority Bus Terminal and Grand Central Station in New York City, varying what he wore slightly. He would stop people and say that he was terribly embarrassed, but he had forgotten his wallet and needed seventy-five cents to get home. He did this for one hour wearing a suit but no tie. Then he panhandled a second hour with one little change: he wore the same suit but added a necktie. In the first hour, he collected $7.23. In the second hour, he collected twenty-six dollars, and one man even gave him extra money with which to buy a newspaper.

After conducting hundreds of other studies and experiments over a period of years, Molloy concluded that the success we have in life is directly related to what we wear. Of clothing in general, he concludes, "We all wear uniforms and our uniforms are clear and distinct signs of class. We react to them accordingly."[4] The more professionally we dress, the more respectable and responsible other people perceive us to be. The clothes we wear say something about what we're doing, where we're going, and whom we're planning to see. They reveal our attitudes toward ourselves, toward others, toward our work, and toward God.

Of course, different occasions call for different clothing. For instance, we probably wouldn't wear the same outfit to go picnicking with our family as we would to go to work as a bank manager. Likewise, when we come to worship before the Lord, we wouldn't wear the same clothes that we'd wear if we were going to the beach. Yet some people come to church to worship the King of the cosmos dressed as if they were going to a basketball game or on some other secular outing. If those are the best clothes they own, then they should put them on and come anyway; God will certainly bless them. The point is that when we come before the Lord, we should wear our most respectful clothing—whatever it happens to be.

In Bible times, clothing was often used for identification or to depict status. For example, Jacob gave Joseph a multi-colored robe (Genesis 37:3), which apparently was an ancient symbol for royalty and was given only to very special children. (King David's daughters wore coats of many colors; see 2 Samuel 13:18.)

In the New Testament, we find that John the Baptist stood out in the crowd because he wore very plain, modest clothing in a day when the political and religious leaders loved to wear ornaments and long, flowing robes. Mark 1:6 says that John wore a robe of camel hair and a leather belt around his waist. It's no wonder that the Jews who saw John were reminded of the prophet Elijah, whom the Old Testament describes as being similarly garbed (see 2 Kings 1:8). And Revelation mentions two women, one of whom represents God's church, and the other an apostate, or fallen, church. These women never actually speak. Not once does the Bible depict them opening their mouths to utter a word. Yet we can easily identify who they are because the Bible tells us what they're wearing as well as what they're doing (Revelation 12:1, 2, 5, 6; 17:1–6).

The very fact that clothing is used as identification leads us to an important point. As Christians, we shouldn't wear anything that might give someone the wrong impression of what kind of God we serve.

So, what shall we wear?

In the Bible, clothing is used metaphorically too. The Bible mentions several things we should remember to wear. One thing everybody should put on is a smile. Many of us could do a lot more to advertise for Jesus simply by looking happier. Too many Christians go around looking like they've been baptized in vinegar—and then they wonder why their family and friends aren't interested in hearing their testimony. I believe that many more people would want to be Christians if we would just look more positive and happy about our relationship with Jesus.

Ephesians 6:11 says we also need to "put on the whole amour of God, that ye may be able to stand against the wiles of the devil" (KJV). God supplies it for us, but you and I must make time to put it on each day. And God's armor is more than an imaginary covering.

You've probably heard or read Hans Christian Anderson's classic fairy tale "The Emperor's New Clothes." In this charming story, a pair of unscrupulous tailors take advantage of the vain emperor's love for fancy threads. They claim that they have invented a method to weave a cloth so light and fine that it looks invisible to all who are too stupid and incompetent to appreciate its quality. They then "present" the emperor with garments made of this cloth, which of course he can't see. Not wanting his courtiers to think him ignorant, however, the emperor pretends to admire the fine workmanship and beautiful colors of the clothes. Then the scoundrels encourage the emperor to make a grand procession through the city to show off his beautiful new garments. He does so, and the people, also not wanting to look like fools, praise the beauty of what he's wearing. Finally, a little boy in the crowd of onlookers points out what everyone can plainly see. He shouts, "The emperor isn't wearing any clothes!" While the people roar with laughter, the king continues his charade parade.

However when we talk about the armor of God, we aren't simply describing fantasy clothes. The Bible says that we are to wear the belt of truth, the breastplate of righteousness, gospel shoes, the shield of faith, the helmet of salvation, and the sword of the Spirit (Ephesians 6:14–17). These are real principles that we must put on by faith each day. We do this, for example, by putting the Word of God in our hearts and our minds and by taking it wherever we go. These various implements really do work. They are exactly what Jesus used to combat the devil in the wilderness of temptation (Luke 4:1–13), and they are available for us everyday. When we forget to wear them, we soon know how real they are!

If we're going to be effective in saving others, we need to be properly clad. Romans 13:12 tells us: "The night is far spent, the day is at hand. Therefore let us cast off the works of darkness, and let us put on the armor of light." Jesus said that people ought to look at us and see that we've got an inner glow. "Let your light so shine before men, that they may see your good works and glorify your Father in heaven" (Matthew 5:16).

Does it matter what we wear?

Jesus shared a parable about a king who planned a wedding feast. At most weddings today, the bridesmaids buy their own dresses and the groomsmen rent their own tuxedoes. However, at some of the more lavish weddings, the couple's sponsors will buy all of the dresses and pay for the tuxedoes. When a king has a wedding for his son, you can be sure that he supplies the necessary garments. That was understood in this parable, especially when you consider that the king had to go out in the highways and the byways and the hedges to get people to come to the wedding banquet. Those poor people certainly didn't have appropriate wedding garments for a royal wingding.

That is why it's incredible that someone dared to show up without the wedding garment the king had supplied. When asked how he could have been so careless, the man was speechless (see Matthew 22:12). He had no excuse. The king had purchased a garment for him; he simply didn't take the time or energy to don the garment that had been provided at great cost. Consequently, the king said to his servants, "Bind him hand and foot, take him away, and cast him into outer darkness; there will be weeping and gnashing of teeth" (verse 13).

This parable is especially relevant for us today because it's important for us to be wearing the right type of clothing when Jesus comes. Scripture tells us that He's coming soon for His special bride. "As Christ also loved the church, and gave himself for it; that he might sanctify and cleanse it with the washing of water by the word, that he might present it to himself a glorious church, not having spot, or wrinkle, or any such thing; but that it should be holy and without blemish" (Ephesians 5:25–27, KJV).

Ever since the creation of Adam and Eve, the devil has been seeking to strip and humiliate the children of God. When the prodigal son came home, his father had the best robe he owned brought out to cover his son's dirty, humiliating rags. So, when we come to our loving Father, He receives us with open arms and brings out the best robe in the universe—Jesus' robe of righteousness—to cover our sins.

Perhaps you're wondering how you can obtain those perfect garments of Christ. Jesus said, "I counsel thee to buy of me gold tried in the fire, that thou mayest be rich; and white raiment, that thou mayest be clothed, and that the shame of thy nakedness do not appear" (Revelation 3:18, KJV). Our pure white garments come from Jesus. He doesn't charge a high price for them—salvation is a free gift (see Romans 6:23). The Lord wants nothing but the gold of our faith and the silver of our love. "He that hath no money; come ye, buy, . . . without money and without price" (Isaiah 55:1, KJV). "If God so clothes the grass of the field, which today is, and tomorrow is, thrown into the oven, will He not much more clothe you, O you of little faith?" (Matthew 6:30).

You might also be thinking, *I'm afraid to wear this spotless white garment—I might get it dirty. If I make a mistake, how do I clean that robe and keep it clean?* Revelation 7:14 gives us the answer—our garments can be washed in the blood of the Lamb. When we come to Jesus, and we can come just as we are, He gives us a spotless white robe of righteousness as a gift, which we accept by faith. This is justification. Sanctification is the next step. It's a process in which we learn how to keep that robe clean. However, Jesus' blood is a powerful stain remover that He'll use when we slip and fall and soil our robe. "If we confess our sins, He is faithful and just to forgive us our sins and to cleanse us from all unrighteousness" (1 John 1:9). His blood is readily available, but it is infinitely precious, so we don't want to carelessly soil the pure robes He gives us.

Laundromat closed

Many of us have had easy access to a washer and dryer our entire lives, but others haven't. Washing one's clothes is quite a chore when one has to beat them on a rock by some river or lake. Once, the clothes washer at our cabin in the hills broke down while we were vacationing there. I found myself wearing the same things for several days because I didn't want to go to the trouble of washing them by hand. I also began to be a little more careful to keep my clothes clean since I knew how much work it would be to clean them.

Because the grace of God is so abundant and His mercy is so near at hand, we are sometimes inclined to take them for granted. There is a risk that we can abuse His mercy. Paul asks, "Shall we continue in sin, that grace may abound? God forbid. How shall we, that are dead to sin, live any longer therein?" (Romans 6:1, 2, KJV).

I believe the Lord wants to teach us how to keep the apparel He provides clean forever. Many of us are waiting for some sort of special infusion of the Spirit to be administered in the future that will miraculously enable us to live victorious lives, but it has actually already been delivered. On the Day of Pentecost, Jesus sent His Spirit, and He has never retracted it.

The grace of Jesus is constantly available today so our sins can be washed away whenever we ask Him to do it. We too often forget that this cleansing won't always be available. A day is coming when Jesus will proclaim from the heavens that the "laundry" is closed. "He which is filthy, let him be filthy still: and he that is righteous, let him be righteous still" (Revelation 22:11, KJV).

Perhaps, like me, you're filled with amazement at God's generosity and can't comprehend how a life that has been so filthy can be suddenly washed spotlessly clean. Remember that "with God all things are possible" (Matthew 19:26). The Bible says, "Put on the whole armor" (Ephesians 6:11), "Buy from Me . . . white garments" (Revelation 3:18), and "Put on Christ" (Galatians 3:27). God is inviting us to take action—to wear these things He has provided. In so doing, we will be putting on the characteristics of Christ and thus revealing His character.

---

1. High-Tech Productions, "NASA Apollo 11-Neil Armstrong Spacesuit," High-Tech Productions, http://www.hightechscience.org/apollo_spacesuit.htm (accessed May 3, 2010).

2. Urban Dictionary, "Urban Dictionary, Wardrobe Malfunction," Urban Dictionary, http://www.urbandictionary.com/define.php?term=wardrobe+malfunction

3. Eric Alterman, *Why We're Liberals: A Political Handbook for Post-Bush America* (New York: Penguin USA, 2008), 186, quoted in Wikipedia, "Wardrobe malfunction," Wikipedia, http://en.wikipedia.org/w/index.php?title=Wardrobe_malfunction&oldid=357318072 (accessed May 3, 2010).

4. John T. Molloy, *John T. Molloy's New Dress for Success* (New York: Warner Books, 1988), 29.

Chapter 8
You Are What You Think

As he thinketh in his heart, so is he.

—Proverbs 23:7, KJV

Your brain weighs only about three pounds, yet it is believed that the total information storage capacity of all its synapses is somewhere around one thousand terabytes—or one hundred times more information than in all the printed books in the Library of Congress. To put that in perspective, it would take more than 23,400 DVDs to store all the information that your brain is capable of holding![1] Modern medicine likewise understands much more about the human heart than about the brain. The human mind is truly the last frontier on earth.

If you could put a price on your brain, how much do you think it would be worth? Well, Thomas Edison got thousands of patents in his lifetime. Around the time of his death, an economic analyst for the *New York Times* estimated that the brain of this notable genius was worth twenty-five billion dollars, which the analyst derived largely from the business interests resulting from his inventions.

In order for us to know who we really are, we need to think about what we think about. If you are anything like me, you rarely think about your thinking. And sadly, for most of us, thinking usually just happens; it resembles a ship that goes wherever the wind blows it because it doesn't have an anchor or a rudder. Rarely do we focus our thinking as did Thomas Edison. I think we should challenge ourselves to think more about what we think about.

If we can learn to play the piano or speak a second language, we can also train our minds to think well in just about every circumstance. And this is absolutely crucial as we head into the last days of earth's history: we need to have strong, sharp minds that are ready to recognize and refute the devil's challenges.

Our ability to reason in abstract ways is perhaps the most fundamental difference between human beings and the rest of God's animal creation. And it is a significant difference, because someday we will answer to God for what we choose to think. "The LORD does not see as man sees; for man looks at the outward appearance, but the LORD looks at the heart" (1 Samuel 16:7). So, even if we can fool others with our so-called righteous actions and we entertain sin only in our minds and enjoy the pleasures of those forbidden escapades with our imaginations alone, God still sees it. He knows where our hearts lie. And as the book of Proverbs tells us, it's what we think in our hearts that counts—that reveals the real person.

Before the Hoover Dam was built, billions of gallons of rainwater would rampage down the Colorado River and rush out to the sea. But once that water was controlled, it was available for drinking, for the irrigation of millions of acres of farmland, and for generating a tremendous amount of electricity. Most people let their thoughts flood aimlessly through their minds and out into a sea of oblivion, but under the influence and control of the Holy Spirit, a great deal of good can be accomplished by how we use our thoughts.

Ever since I was a daydreaming child in grade school, I have experienced problems controlling my wild cogitating. I suspect it's a battle we all face, but it is imperative that everyone start thinking about what we think because it matters to God.

Sinful thoughts

Are we really that responsible for what we think? Well, yes and no. Certainly, thoughts tend to run through our minds as if they were on a conveyor belt. Sometimes we can't help what we start thinking, especially with the blizzard of information coming in through our senses that our brains have to sort. Psychologists have estimated that about ten thousand thoughts go through our brains every day. But even then, we can choose what to keep in our brains for processing and what to discard. And a lot of Christians dwell on very unhealthy, very sinful rubbish rather than focusing on that which is holy, good, and true.

Jesus taught that we can commit perjury, murder, and adultery in the mind (see, for example, Matthew 5:28.) He said, "Those things which proceed out of the mouth come from the heart, and they defile a man. For out of the heart proceed evil thoughts, murders, adulteries, fornications, thefts, false witness, blasphemies. These are the things which defile a man" (Matthew 15:18–20). So, according to Jesus, sin always begins in the mind. That's why we can't be indifferent about what we think.

Let me be clear: this doesn't mean that when a tempting thought hits you—for instance, the temptation to shoplift an item from a store—it's necessarily a sin. If I told you not to think of a purple monkey with polka dots, you would be hard-pressed not to think about it. I imagine you are thinking about it right now! There are times when we are unable to control the stimulus around us or the evil suggestions the devil may plant in our thoughts. In a world drenched in shameful advertising and revealing fashions and from which ethics has disappeared, the devil has an easy job in planting the seeds of sin in our minds. If we quickly decide to reject the evil thoughts and evict them from our mind, then we haven't sinned. But when we deliberately choose to dwell on the evil thought and to embrace it, it becomes a sin.

As they say in flying, "your attitude determines your altitude." When you adjust an airplane's attitude—the angle at which the wings hit the air—the plane will either ascend or descend. In the same way, our attitudes toward sin will affect the "altitude" of our lives. If our minds are constantly dwelling on trash, that's where our lives will go. If our attitudes are focused upward, on the spiritual, we will glide up to heaven. Yet God's people are often blasé about the connection between our thoughts and our success as Christians. George Barna, the famous researcher, put it this way: "The vast majority of Christians do not behave differently because they do not think differently."[2]

You are what you see

How does a person become spiritually minded, thinking the thoughts God wants us to think? Part of training the mind is controlling the inputs. We're likely to let our minds slip into sinful thoughts if we're constantly eyeing what passes for entertainment. What we take into our minds will certainly affect what we think. How much more likely is it that you will have a nightmare if you watch a horror flick before going to bed?

It's a question of focus and attention. The reason this is so crucial is that we never really stop thinking, which makes what we think and how we control our thinking so important. Ultimately, we are what we think, and what we think on is largely determined by what we focus on, what we look at. The more poison we let into our minds, the more poison we're likely to process in our thinking and the more poison we're likely to leave in the world.

Isaiah said of the wicked, "Their feet run to evil, and they make haste to shed innocent blood; their thoughts are thoughts of iniquity" (Isaiah 59:7). If our thinking is influenced by what we take into our minds, shouldn't we be particularly careful about what we choose to watch and hear? Some Christians wonder, *Lord, why can't I be more like Christ? Why is the Christian walk so difficult?* Yet they're filling their minds with things that are totally opposed to Christ. We console ourselves that we would never consider murder or adultery or stealing or lying, yet many deliberately choose to do these forbidden behaviors vicariously by beholding entertainment filled with these acts (see Matthew 15:17). That's a startling contradiction. It is, in fact, one of the most dangerous problems in the church virtually everywhere in the world. It's the frivolous, nasty things that people watch and hear and read that vex their minds with filth and temptation. Do not be deceived; God is not mocked. "To be carnally minded is death. . . . Because the carnal mind is enmity against God; for it is not subject to the law of God, neither indeed can be. So then, those who are in the flesh cannot please God" (Romans 8:6–8). What we sow into our minds, we will reap in our thoughts and actions.

You are what you study

Someone once said, "Show me what a man reads and I will tell you what kind of man he is." And Scripture says, "Study to shew thyself approved unto God, a workman that needeth not to be ashamed, rightly dividing the word of truth" (2 Timothy 2:15, KJV). Every believer should dedicate quality time each day to prayer and Bible study. Establish a library of good inspirational books to read and CDs to listen to when you drive. There's an ocean of great material for reading and sermons that you can download from the Internet. There's also some poor stuff, too, so "squeeze the tomatoes" as you shop. Naturally, I recommend www .amazingfacts.org as a place to start. Make this study time as important and regular to you as your daily meals. Job said, "I have esteemed the words of his mouth more than my necessary food" (Job 23:12, KJV). Good study is one of the most practical things you can do to change your thinking.

Real truth requires real thinking. But the average person doesn't crave Bible doctrines that require them to study and think deeply for themselves. They want the pastor to spoon-feed them sweet spiritual Pablum. The book of Hebrews speaks of this: "Though by this time you ought to be teachers, you need someone to teach you again the basic elements of the oracles of God. You need milk, not solid food; for everyone who lives on milk, being still an infant, is unskilled in the word of righteousness. But solid food is for the mature, for those whose faculties have been trained by practice to distinguish good from evil" (Hebrews 5:12–14, NRSV).

Luther Burbank said, "Less than fifteen per cent of the people do any original thinking on any subject. . . . The greatest torture in the world for most people is to think." But God invites us to daily, deliberately discipline our minds to pray, study, and meditate on His truth. As James Allen put it, "Good thoughts bear good fruit, bad thoughts bear bad fruit—and man is his own gardener."

Good Bible study isn't just copious reading or constantly listening to sermon CDs. It requires us to mentally masticate what we've read. As we ponder the biblical truths, the mind files away the thoughts and principles for future application. Good study and prayer must be combined with the processing that meditation provides. Paul instructed Timothy, "Till I come, give attention to reading, to exhortation, to doctrine. . . . Meditate on these things; give yourself entirely to them, that your progress may be evident to all" (1 Timothy 4:13, 15).

Of course, I'm not talking about the Eastern conception of meditation in which people are told to empty their minds. Rather, I'm speaking of the biblical model of meditation, in which we set a truth down in our minds and mentally walk around it, studying its different angles. The best summary description of biblical meditation that I've found is in a famous devotional by Charles Spurgeon. I can't improve on it, so here it is.

"I will meditate in Thy precepts."—Psalm 119:15

There are times when solitude is better than society, and silence is wiser than speech. We should be better Christians if we were more alone, waiting upon God, and gathering through meditation on His Word spiritual strength for labour in His service. We ought to muse *upon the things of God, because we thus get the real nutriment out of them.* Truth is something like the cluster of the vine: if we would have wine from it, we must bruise it; we must press and squeeze it many times. The bruiser's feet must come down joyfully upon the bunches, or else the juice will not flow; and they must well tread the grapes, or else much of the precious liquid will be wasted. So we must, by meditation, tread the clusters of truth, if we would get the wine of consolation therefrom. Our bodies are not supported by merely taking food into the mouth, but the process which really supplies the muscle, and the nerve, and the sinew, and the bone, is the process of digestion. It is by digestion that the outward food becomes assimilated with the inner life. Our souls are not nourished merely by listening awhile to this, and then to that, and then to the other part of divine truth. Hearing, reading, marking, and learning, all require inwardly digesting to complete their usefulness, and the inward digesting of the truth lies for the most part in meditating upon it. Why is it that some Christians, although they hear many sermons, make but slow advances in the divine life? Because they neglect their closets, and do not thoughtfully meditate on God's Word. They love the wheat, but they do not grind it; they would have the corn, but they will not go forth into the fields to gather it; the fruit hangs upon the tree, but they will not pluck it; the water flows at their feet, but they will not stoop to drink it. From such folly deliver us, O Lord, and be this our resolve this morning, "I will meditate in Thy precepts."[3]

Positive thinking

A couple of church elders were trying to figure out why their church wasn't growing. One asked the other, "What do you think our problem is, ignorance or apathy?" The other replied, "I don't know, and I don't care." This attitude summarizes the lukewarm condition of many churches—the members lack knowledge, passion, and purity. How can we expect church members to be zealous about their faith or to think spiritually healthy thoughts if they're constantly feeding on the fodder of the world? Paul outlines the ideal for positive, pure, and holy thinking: "Whatsoever things are true, whatsoever things are honest, whatsoever things are just, whatsoever things are pure, whatsoever things are lovely, whatsoever things are of good report; if there be any virtue, and if there be any praise, think on these things" (Philippians 4:8, KJV).

Romans 8:6 promises, "To be spiritually minded is life and peace." God wants us to be as positive and spiritual in our thinking as possible, and He enables us to think positive thoughts despite our fleshly struggles. That's what real faith is—thinking that God is with us in spite of what we are experiencing. Remember that John Bunyan wrote the inspiring classic *Pilgrim's Progress* while he was in prison. While in the Bedford jail, all he could do was to think, so he consciously decided to use that time to think elevating, productive thoughts, and the book that came from his thinking has transformed countless lives.

We often talk and think based solely on our feelings, but our feelings don't have to dictate what we think. We might get grumpy when we haven't eaten in a while or when we're tired; but I'm not sure that in the judgment, low blood sugar will be a valid excuse for cultivating ugly thoughts. That's why it is better to think and behave based on principles rather than on our feelings. When the devil tempted Jesus in the wilderness, Jesus didn't turn to sinful thinking and excuse it because He was hungry and tired. He didn't allow His physical needs to rule His mind. Instead, He remembered the promises of God's Word and rebuked the devil. That is a tremendous example, one we must strive to imitate. If we could justify our wayward thoughts and actions because of how we're feeling, then we could justify every immoral action, and there would be no need for a life-changing gospel.

Steps to better thinking

So how can we as lowly, selfish humans think the way

God wants us to think? By letting God control our minds. How does that happen? We simply ask and believe. The Holy Spirit is willing to work wonders in our thinking. "Those who live according to the flesh set their minds on the things of the flesh, but those who live according to the Spirit, the things of the Spirit" (Romans 8:5).

Before I accepted Christ, I had a nasty vocabulary. I cursed habitually because I was living in the world, and the world's vocabulary is really terrible. When I invited the Lord into my heart, I noticed that as I'd get ready to say something crude or inappropriate out of habit, God would pull the emergency brake on my tongue. Suddenly, a little voice would whisper, "Don't say that." And I praised the Lord, because I saw with the aid of God's Spirit I was actually in control of my thinking. Well, it was actually the Holy Spirit who was in control and who changed my mind and my talking. God will do that for you, too, if you are willing.

We would all think differently if we would remember the first great commandment: "Thou shalt love the Lord thy God with all thy heart, and with all thy soul, and with all thy mind" (Matthew 22:37, KJV). How do we love the Lord with our minds? I can tell you it isn't by imagining a bouquet of flowers in God's honor. Rather, it is telling Him that we want to think like Him, that we desire the mind of Christ.

God tells us, "My thoughts are not your thoughts, neither are your ways my ways, saith the LORD. For as the heavens are higher than the earth, so are my ways higher than your ways, and my thoughts than your thoughts" (Isaiah 55:8, 9, KJV). So He invites us to think with His mind. "Come now, and let us reason together" (Isaiah 1:18). We see a demonstration of God's thoughts in His two great "books"—the Bible and creation. The universe and every-

Sign up your children for an AMAZING ADVENTURE

The popular *Amazing Adventure Bible Guides* from Amazing Facts are now available for **FREE**! Created for kids ages 8 to 12, these educational lessons will take your children on an adventure with Jesus through the Bible! The lessons include colorful pictures, puzzles, and a path paved in Bible verses that will lead your children on an incredible journey to find the treasures of truth on Bible topics such as salvation, heaven, hell, and baptism.

▼ To enroll your child, fill in this card and drop it in the mail. *

Parent's Name _____

Child's Name _____ Child's Age ☐

Address _____

City _____

State _____ ZIP Code _____

☐ English
☐ Español

*You can also enroll your child online at **amazingbiblestudies.com/by-mail.** Under the "Course" drop-down menu, choose: "English - Amazing Adventure (for Children)."

Free offer available in North America and U.S. territories only.

M1575

INTERNATIONAL
P.O. Box 909
Roseville, CA 95678-0909

thing we see in the world are examples of God's thoughts, with all of their magnificent wonder and beauty. Spend more time in nature. Surrounded by His creation, you will find yourself echoing His thoughts.

The other way to think God's thoughts, as I've already mentioned, is to commit ourselves to prayer and Bible study. Just as pop culture can infect our thinking with all kinds of empty, carnal thoughts, so the Bible can infuse our thinking with holy and spiritual thoughts. If instead of watching that movie or TV program, we'll covenant with God to read His Word, we'll soon see how quickly the Holy Spirit can change our thinking.

> Oh, how I love Your law!
> It is my meditation all the day.
> You, through Your commandments, make me wiser than my enemies;
> For they are ever with me.
> I have more understanding than all my teachers,
> For Your testimonies are my meditation (Psalm 119:97–99).

A new positive pattern of thinking is one of the best signs that God is transforming our hearts. "Who has the heart? With whom are our thoughts? Of whom do we love to converse? Who has our warmest affections and our best energies? If we are Christ's, our thoughts are with Him, and our sweetest thoughts are of Him. All we have and are is consecrated to Him. We long to bear His image, breathe His spirit, do His will, and please Him in all things."[4]

Fall in love again

Thomas Traherne correctly mused that "as nothing is

more easy than to think, so nothing is more difficult than to think well."[5] It will certainly take effort to experience any change in our thinking, but God will help us if we ask Him. "Search me, O God, and know my heart: try me, and know my thoughts: and see if there be any wicked way in me, and lead me in the way everlasting" (Psalm 139:23, KJV). The renewal of our minds is a process that requires time. But we are commanded to eventually cast "down arguments and every high thing that exalts itself against the knowledge of God, bringing every thought into captivity to the obedience of Christ" (2 Corinthians 10:5).

Bring "every thought into captivity"? Is such a command even reasonable?

When we have the Holy Spirit and the mind of Christ, it is. When we're totally in love with someone, we don't have to try to think about that person. Dwelling on the person we love is a natural, spontaneous behavior. The heart is a magnet drawn toward what it loves. When we love the Lord with all our minds, we will find ourselves thinking about Him all the time—thinking about Him and what He desires rather than what the world desires. Only then can we bring every thought into captivity to Christ.

You won't attract doves to your backyard with roadkill. That will only bring in the vultures. But if you fill a feeder with birdseed, provide a clean birdbath, and build an elevated nest shelter, there's a good chance some doves will show up.

We can't make the miracle of conversion happen by doing good works, but it won't come if we feed on what the world has for us to consume. We can provide an inviting environment for the Spirit by what we choose to read, watch, and talk about. Conversion happens with the renewing of our minds, which the Holy Spirit makes possible so we can "prove what is that good and acceptable and perfect will of God" (Romans 12:2). As mentioned earlier, we have to put off the old self of Ephesians 4:22–24, "which grows corrupt according to the deceitful lusts, and be renewed in the spirit of your mind, and that you put on the new man which was created according to God, in true righteousness and holiness."

God is offering us that new covenant—the new heart He wants to put within us. And it is a wonderful thing, because "blessed are the pure in heart"—pure in thought and mind—"for they shall see God" (Matthew 5:8). Not a single atom of your body is going to make it to heaven, not even your brain matter. What's going to go? Your thoughts, your character, which will be downloaded into a new body. So it really is important what you think about.

Are you beginning to think about what you are thinking about?

1. Robert Birge, Syracuse University, 1996.

2. George Barna, *The Second Coming of the Church* (Nashville, Tenn.: Word Publishing, 1998), 122.

3. Charles Spurgeon, *Morning and Evening: A Contemporary Version of a Devotional Classic Based on the King James Version* (Peabody, Mass.: Hendrickson Publisher, 1991), Morning, October 12; emphasis in original.

4. Ellen G. White, *Steps to Christ* (Washington, D.C.: Review and Herald®, 1956), 58.

5. Thomas Traherne, *Centuries of Meditation,* ed. Bertram Dobell (London: n.p., 1908), http://books.google.com/books?id=K-gTAAAA YAAJ&pg=PA4&dq=Thomas+Traherne++Centuries+of+Meditations& cd=1#v=onepage&q&f=false (accessed May 5, 2010).

Chapter 9
What Should You Do With Guilt?

Beloved, if our heart does not condemn us,
we have confidence toward God.

—1 John 3:21

Have you ever taken your foot off the gas pedal when you saw a highway patrol officer? You might even have hit the brakes though you were actually going under the speed limit. Why? Might it be because you often break the speed limit and you fear that you might be speeding now?

There are times when feeling guilty is a good thing. If we are violating our consciences or being knowingly disobedient, we *should* be troubled. If we never feel guilt, something is probably wrong with our redemption radar. The Bible says, "There is not a just man upon earth, that doeth good, and sinneth not" (Ecclesiastes 7:20, KJV).

Of course, no one enjoys guilt; yet everyone who has a normal, healthy conscience experiences it. It shouldn't surprise us, though, that popular philosophies and even some trendy theologies clamor that all guilt is bad. Feel-good preachers say we should try to prevent any guilt from troubling our minds, no matter what we're doing. If we actually do this, we can grieve away the Holy Spirit. Paul wrote about people "having their own conscience seared with a hot iron" (1 Timothy 4:2). And he warned, "Do not grieve the Holy Spirit of God, by whom you were sealed for the day of redemption" (Ephesians 4:30). No matter how stressful or uncomfortable guilt can be, feeling guilty isn't always a bad thing.

Obviously, it would be nice to live without pain. But the nerves that give us pain keep us alive. Hansen's disease—what used to be called leprosy—attacks a person's nervous system and can eventually kill the feeling in the extremities. When people with this disease touch a hot stove, they don't feel the heat or the pain, so they burn their fingers. Eventually, with enough such incidents, they may lose their fingers. Amazingly, Hansen's disease even disrupts the blinking reflex—the impression that tells us to lubricate our eyes. So those with this disease are subject to dry eyes and thus are susceptible to eye infections and blindness. Sensations of discomfort and pain are actually a blessing.[1]

Likewise, while guilt doesn't feel good, it keeps our conscience alive. Jesus called the Holy Spirit a Comforter, but that same Spirit also convicts the world of its sin (see John 16:8). We know the Holy Spirit is working in our lives when the sensation of guilt follows bad behavior on our part. Remorse for sin is often a wonderful sign from God of new spiritual life!

Responding to guilt

Have you ever been gossiping with someone when unexpectedly the very person you're discussing walks into the room? You suddenly get very quiet and perhaps mumble something about the weather. Why that reaction? Guilt. Is that a good or bad reaction? Probably good. You *should* be ashamed if you're engaging in gossip!

When Peter preached that Spirit-filled sermon during Pentecost, one of the signs that his message was effective is found in how his listeners responded. "They were pricked in their heart." They were convicted, and they pleaded, "What shall we do?" (Acts 2:37, KJV).

That was a good response. After Isaiah saw God, he cried out, "Woe is me, for I am undone! Because I am a man of unclean lips" (Isaiah 6:5). When Isaiah saw God's holiness and goodness, he became aware of the evil in his heart, and then God cleansed him of his sin. Only after people sense their guilt do they realize their need for forgiveness. Only when the hearts of the people who heard Peter preach were humbled by conviction could he talk to them about repentance and forgiveness.

The closer we draw to Christ, the more frequently we'll experience moments of guilt. That might sound like a paradox, but it's true. The nearer we come to the Light, the more clearly we'll see the blemishes in our life—flaws that we may never have noticed before. So, when we live in view of the holiness of Jesus, we're likely to feel a sense of guilt and shame. But when we sincerely repent and ask for forgiveness, we'll experience grace and peace. "Humble yourselves in the sight of the Lord, and He will lift you up" (James 4:10).

John 8 contains the well-known story of a woman caught in adultery. Her accusers stand by to condemn her, saying to Jesus, "Moses in the law commanded us, that such should be stoned: but what sayest thou?" (verse 5, KJV). Jesus ignores their sharp accusations and stoops down to write in the dust on the temple floor. When the accusers continue to press their case, Jesus straightens up and says, "He that is without sin among you, let him first cast a stone at her" (verse 7, KJV). Then He returns to His writing. The Bible says, "They which heard it, being convicted by their own conscience, went out one by one, beginning at the eldest, even unto the last" (verse 9, KJV). They felt guilt, and they walked away.

What was Jesus writing as the accusers sought to get

Him to condemn the woman? I believe that He was writing down the laws that these very men had themselves broken. Then, as each one was convicted about his own guilt, he left.

Sometimes, however, the guilty react in anger when they are convicted. When the religious leaders heard Stephen's powerfully convicting sermon, they were so troubled that they stopped listening and then stoned him to death (see Acts 7:57–59).

When we're angry at someone else, we need to pause and ask ourselves if we're angry because of that person's wrongdoing or because we're convicted that he or she may be right. Is that person simply reminding us of our guilt? In fact, many people avoid church because they want to avoid places that stir the unpleasant sensations of shame. That's like a person with toothaches and multiple cavities refusing to go to the dentist because he or she is afraid of the novocaine shot.

The heart of guilt

One of the best possible goals we can have is to go through life feeling that we are at peace with God—that we stand before Him in innocence. Job declares, "My righteousness I hold fast, and will not let it go; my heart shall not reproach me as long as I live" (Job 27:6).

The Bible says Job was a perfect and upright man who feared God and hated evil, but I don't think he claimed to be sinless. Why then could he say that his heart wasn't condemning him? Because whenever he became aware of any sin, he dealt with it quickly, keeping his account with God up to date. He sacrificed for himself and his family every day, so his conscience was always clear before the Lord.

Have you ever felt condemned by your own heart? Sometimes it hits us like a bolt of lightning. Other times it might build slowly, as if we know we're doing something wrong but are trying to ignore it, until it begins to boil over and suddenly we have an awful revelation when we see ourselves through God's eyes. We feel guilty and condemned, and like David, we cry, "I have sinned" (2 Samuel 12:13). We must first tell the Lord our problems. Next we must ask the Lord to help us stop committing that sin. Then we can know who we are—that we are people who stand forgiven and innocent before His eyes.

What a wonderful thing when, as was true of Job, our hearts no longer condemn us. "Beloved, if our heart does not condemn us, we have confidence toward God" (1 John 3:21). And who has the authority—the temerity—to condemn us when "Christ who died, and furthermore is also risen, who is even at the right hand of God, . . . makes intercession for us" (Romans 8:34)?

But there is someone who condemns us even when we are forgiven and right with God.

The pain of phantom guilt

Amputees often experience a sensation called "phantom pain." For example, they might have lost their entire left leg in some accident, but they may feel that the toes on their left foot hurt or their left knee itches even though those body parts are gone. Doctors are helpless—unable to treat this part of the body that is screaming for attention even though it no longer exists. In the same way, there are many Christians, new and old, who have confessed and forsaken their sins and applied the blood of Jesus for cleansing, yet still feel the phantom pain of guilt. They believe God has forgiven them but they haven't forgiven themselves.

It has been said that the devil appeared to Martin Luther once, carrying a scroll that contained an extensive inventory of Luther's sins. The devil said, "Do you really think that God can forgive all this? You're a doomed man."

Luther saw the list and thought, *There's no hope for me.* But then he noticed that the devil's hand was covering some words at the top of the scroll, so he asked, "What is your hand covering?"

The devil answered, "Nothing," and pointed to the chronicle of Luther's sins again.

But Luther demanded, "In the name of Jesus, remove your hand!" And when the devil took his hand away, Luther could see the words *All under the blood.* Then, defeated and angry, the devil had to retreat.

Satan will often seek to discourage us by dredging up our past and every shameful thing we've said and done. He'll exhume the sins we've buried at the cross and present them to us in the most hopeless context, trying once again to bind this heavy burden on our backs. Sometimes he'll do this through church members. When he does this to you, rebuke him in Jesus' name and repeat the promises in God's Word. Remember that Jesus came

to loose the bonds of wickedness,
To undo the heavy burdens,
To let the oppressed go free,
And . . . break every yoke (Isaiah 58:6).

An old man was carrying a large sack of potatoes to the market in town. A kind farmer stopped and offered him a ride in his wagon. When the weathered man had struggled into the back of the cart, the farmer noticed that he was still holding the sack of potatoes on his shoulder. "Friend," the farmer said, "set down your load and rest your back." But the weary fellow responded, "Mister, you were kind enough to give me a ride. I wouldn't dare ask you to carry my sack of potatoes too."

Of course, we know the worn traveler was silly not to put down his load and rest, yet there are millions of Christians who accept Jesus' forgiving mercy but feel they must continue to carry their burdens of guilt and shame. Far too many of God's children are struggling through life, dragging around this worse-than-useless burden.

Paul wrote, "Let us lay aside every weight, and the sin which so easily ensnares us, and let us run with endurance the race that is set before us, looking unto Jesus, the author and finisher of our faith" (Hebrews 12:1, 2). To successfully run this race, we are commanded to lay aside not only our sins, but also the weight of guilt that impedes us. Scripture tells us that "if we confess our sins, He is faithful and just to forgive us our sins and to cleanse us from all unrighteousness" (1 John 1:9). That cleansing removes the guilt of sin. Let's believe God's promise and avoid the pain of phantom guilt.

---

1. *Mycobacterium leprae and leprosy: a compendium*, 729–736.

Chapter 10
What Do You Think You're Worth?

Of how much more value . . . is a man than a sheep?
—Matthew 12:12

What is the value of a human body?

Certainly we're worth more alive than dead, but even the raw materials in our bodies have some value. The U.S. Bureau of Chemistry and Soils has calculated the chemical and mineral composition of the human body. It breaks down as follows: 65 percent oxygen, 18 percent carbon, 10 percent hydrogen, 3 percent nitrogen, 1.5 percent calcium, 1 percent phosphorous, 0.35 percent potassium, 0.25 percent sulfur, 0.15 percent sodium, 0.15 percent chlorine, 0.05 percent magnesium, 0.0004 percent iron, and 0.00004 percent iodine. Our bodies also contain trace quantities of fluorine, silicon, manganese, zinc, copper, aluminum, and arsenic.[1] Rendered down to these simple elements, our bodies are worth just a few dollars. However, in terms of the adrenaline, insulin, growth hormones, and other complex chemicals and hormones in our bodies, they're worth a lot more. And of course body parts used in transplants are worth thousands if the donors are healthy. Let's hope you don't have to discover your real worth based on this criterion!

It's impossible to fully separate who you think you are from what you think you're worth. People's sense of self-worth will be demonstrated a thousand ways in their behavior. The world may measure success by the kind of car a man drives. God is much more concerned with the kind of man who's driving the car. The world stares and chatters over the dress a woman wears. God is more interested in the kind of woman who's wearing the dress. Many families work for years, spend fortunes, and assume staggering debts to own beautiful homes in grand neighborhoods. God is more interested that they become great families with new hearts abiding in Him. The world wants to know how much you earn. God asks how much you give. The world measures your success by how many people work for you. Jesus measures your success by how many people you serve. So, how much do you think you're worth to God?

I love the following quote from *The Desire of Ages*.

Christ pointed to the birds flying in the heavens, to the flowers of the field, and bade His hearers consider these objects of God's creation. "Are not ye of much more value than they?" He said. Matt. 6:26, R. V. The measure of divine attention bestowed on any object is proportionate to its rank in the scale of being. The little brown sparrow is watched over by Providence. The flowers of the field, the grass that carpets the earth, share the notice and care of our heavenly Father. The great Master Artist has taken thought for the lilies, making them so beautiful that they outshine the glory of Solomon. How much more does He care for man, who is the image and glory of God. He longs to see His children reveal a character after His similitude.[2]

Jesus said, "Are not five sparrows sold for two copper coins? And not one of them is forgotten before God. But the very hairs of your head are all numbered. Do not fear therefore; you are of more value than many sparrows" (Luke 12:6, 7). But just what are we worth? The best way to determine something's value is by finding out what will people pay for it. If Christ made all things, then His life would be the most valuable currency in the cosmos—and that's what He paid for us, for you. He became a human being and then exchanged His life for your salvation.

Precious stone

There are expert antique appraisers who travel around and evaluate what others might think is useless junk. The appraisers know that with a little tender care and restoration, some of the things they find can become treasures. For instance, a brooch that was purchased for fourteen dollars at a Bristol, Rhode Island, antique shop, turned out to contain priceless purple pearls. An antiques dealer found the ornamental pin while rummaging through a basket of costume jewelry at an old antique shop. Alan Golash, who restores antique jewelry, cleaned the brooch, and discovered that it was made of 18-karat gold and enamel and included three small rose-cut diamonds. But most notably, the brooch features two rare purple pearls, the larger of which is about the size of a marble. Gem experts say that both of the pearls are completely natural. They're produced by a type of clam known as quahog, which are extraordinarily uncommon. The value of this brooch may exceed a million dollars.[3] Can you imagine selling something for fourteen dollars that you later learn is worth millions? Countless people do this with their own lives every day.

A banker in Chicago always tossed a coin into the cup of a legless beggar who sat on the street outside the bank. But unlike most people, the banker would always insist on getting one of the pencils the man had for sale. "You're a merchant," the banker would say, "and I always expect to receive good value from merchants with whom I do business."

One day the legless man wasn't in his usual place on the sidewalk when the banker came by. Nor was he there on the days that followed. Time passed and the banker forgot about him, until he walked into a public building and there in a concession stand sat the former beggar. He was the owner of his own stationery business now. "I have always hoped you might come by someday," he told the banker. "You're largely responsible for my being here. You kept telling me that I was a merchant. I started thinking of myself that way instead of as a beggar receiving gifts. I started selling pencils—lots of them. You gave me self-respect and caused me to see myself differently."

At an auction of Marilyn Monroe's valuables held in 1999, the dress she wore when she sang "Happy Birthday" to President Kennedy in 1962 sold for $1,267,500.[4] That was the most anyone had ever paid for a dress up to that time—and probably since then. The amount bid for this white silk evening dress covered with 6,000 rhinestone beads and sequins far exceeded the previous record of $222,500 paid for a dark blue velvet dress that Princess Diana wore at a 1985 White House dinner. "We really got the bargain of the century," said Peter Siegel, the New York memorabilia dealer who bought Monroe's dress. "We were prepared to go much higher."

One point two million dollars for a skimpy dress! Yet this is nothing compared to what Jesus paid for us when He purchased our freedom from sin and its penalty with His own blood. The breastplate of Israel's high priest contained threads of gold and was bejeweled with twelve precious stones containing the names of the tribes of Israel (see Exodus 28:15–21). This was a symbol reminding us that Jesus, our High Priest, values us as His greatest treasure and holds our names near to His heart.

The fireproof mansions God is preparing for the redeemed will be covered with glimmering gold and gems. Looking forward to the Messianic kingdom, God has said, "I will make your pinnacles of rubies, your gates of crystal, and all your walls of precious stones" (Isaiah 54:12). And of the New Jerusalem, the capital city of the earth made new, John said, "The foundations of the wall of the city were adorned with all kinds of precious stones" (Revelation 21:19).

In the meantime, the Lord still has an earthly temple here: His church, His people, adorned with precious living stones and gold for beauty. It is living human gems that are the building materials of God's church. "Coming to Him as to a living stone, rejected indeed by men, but chosen by God and precious, you also, as living stones, are being built up a spiritual house, a holy priesthood, to offer up spiritual sacrifices acceptable to God through Jesus Christ" (1 Peter 2:4, 5).

I once read an interesting story about a rather rough, uncultured bachelor. This man fell in love with a beautiful, expensive vase, which he saw in a shop window as he went to and from work each day. Eventually, the man bought this exquisite vase and put it on the mantel by a window. There, its beauty contrasted starkly with the neglected room, and it became a bold judgment on its frumpy surroundings. The man soon felt he had to clean up the room to make it worthy of the vase. The curtains looked drab and faded beside it. The old chair with the stuffing peeking through the covering no longer fit in. The peeling wallpaper and paint fairly shouted their need for renewal. Gradually, one project at a time, the bachelor had the room and then the whole house renovated, until all had been transformed by the introduction of this one valuable and beautiful object. When we recognize the beauty and priceless value of Christ and invite Him into our hearts, He begins to redecorate our lives until we experience an extreme and total makeover. Imagine what that does to our value!

What is your ransom value?

In his book *Open the Door Wide to Happy Living,* T. Huffman Harris told of a discouraged young man named Eddie who became tired of life and one cloudy day decided to end it all by leaping from a bridge into a turbulent river. Jim, a total stranger, was passing by, saw Eddie being swept downstream. Without hesitation he plunged into the water in a selfless effort to save him.

Eddie noticed his would-be rescuer floundering desperately in the strong current and knew that without his help the man would drown. Something stirred within him, and with all his strength, Eddie swam over to the man and rescued him.

Saving the stranger who had attempted to save him brought Eddie new hope and meaning. He had a new concept of what his life was worth because someone else was willing to sacrifice his life to save him.[5] It is only in the light of Christ's sacrifice that we can even begin to appreciate how much we are worth to God. The Father unlocked the vault of heaven and emptied it to save you.

In many parts of the world, kidnapping is on the rise. According to insurance carrier AIG, there are more than twenty thousand kidnap-for-ransom incidents reported annually, 48 percent of which occur in Latin America. Some of these kidnap victims are held for months or even years.

When the sixteen-year-old grandson of oil tycoon Jean Paul Getty was kidnapped in Rome on July 10, 1973, the billionaire hesitated paying the seventeen million dollar ransom demanded for his safe return. In the midst of this tragedy, an Italian postal strike delayed communication. Then an envelope containing a lock of the boy's hair, part of one ear, and a threatening message was delivered to a local newspaper. They now demanded only

3.2 million dollars. The senior Getty negotiated a deal and got his grandson back for about 2.8 million dollars.

How much ransom would you pay to redeem your child or grandchild if, heaven forbid, they were kidnapped? While this is difficult for me to even think about, I would like to believe I would give everything to reclaim my captive child.

It's sad when someone pays a costly ransom and the kidnap victim is never recovered. This was the case in the famous kidnapping of the baby son of Charles Lindbergh. But it's even sadder when people who are victims of the devil's kidnapping, reject the freedom bought for them by the precious blood of Jesus—like Patty Hearst, the granddaughter of publishing magnate William Randolph Hearst. When the ransom was paid for her release, she joined her kidnappers in advancing their cause and even helped them to rob a bank.

The sacrifice of God's Son has provided an abundant ransom, sufficient to redeem all people from their spiritual captivity. How it must break the heart of our heavenly Father when, after He has paid so much to liberate us from Satan's captivity, so many choose to stay in bondage and even join the archfiend in his rebellion.

---

1. H. A. Harper, V. W. Rodwell, P. A. Mayes, *Review of Physiological Chemistry* (Los Altos, Calif.: Lange Medical Publications, University Medical Publishers, 1953).

2. Ellen G. White, *The Desire of Ages* (Mountain View, Calif.: Pacific Press®, 1940), 313.

3. Robert Genis, "The Purple Pearl," *Gemstone Forecaster* 23, no. 2 (Summer 2005), http://www.preciousgemstones.com/gfsummer05.html#4 (accessed May 5, 2010).

4. *Reno Gazette Journal,* August 12, 2004.

5. T. Huffman Harris, *Open the Door Wide to Happy Living* (New York: Carlton Press, 1985).

Chapter 11
Who Has Real Peace?

Peace I leave with you, My peace I give to you;
not as the world gives do I give to you.
Let not your heart be troubled, neither let it be afraid.

—John 14:27

Do you know what led to the creation of the prestigious Nobel Prize? Alfred Nobel invented safety blasting powder, better known as dynamite. It's five times more potent than gunpowder and has made the use of explosives in construction far safer, more efficient, and cheaper than it had been with gun powder and nitroglycerin.

Alfred hoped dynamite would make wars so horrible that people would give them up. Then his brother died, and a newspaper mistakenly published Alfred's obituary instead of his brother's. When Alfred read it, he realized how he'd be remembered when he died—as the man whose invention caused tremendous carnage. So in his will he stipulated that upon his death, the bulk of his vast fortune was to go to a fund that would, every year, celebrate advancements in the sciences, literature, and peace.

Ultimately, everyone desires peace. Many are longing for political peace. Others are craving mental, financial, social, and even physical peace. And most of the world seems to believe that some change in external circumstances is what will bring lasting peace.

In Mark 4, we read the familiar story of the time when, while traveling in a boat across the Lake of Galilee, Jesus slept through a violent storm. Strong winds had arisen, and waves were beating into the boat. But in the stern of the boat, His head on a pillow, Jesus slept on. His disciples, fearing for their lives, awoke Him, and "He arose and rebuked the wind, and said to the sea, 'Peace, be still!' And the wind ceased and there was a great calm" (verse 39).

This is a fascinating tale because it tells us that when the disciples first awakened Jesus, they asked Him a very strange question: "Do You not care that we are perishing?" (verse 38). Of course He cared! He said He came to earth because God so loved the world that He didn't want anyone to perish.

The raging elements didn't distress Jesus. He didn't need to shout to still them; His simple words, spoken in faith, were potent enough.

Curiously, though Jesus had saved the disciples from the raging storm, they were still "exceedingly" afraid (verse 41). Why? After all, the storm was gone and the elements were at peace. It's clear, then, that the fear they felt at this point had nothing to do with the environment. Something else was taking away their peace—something on the inside. The disciples were afraid now because they were wondering, "What manner of man is this, that even the wind and the sea obey him?" (verse 41, KJV). They didn't know Jesus.

Like the disciples, we become anxious and lose faith when the gales blow. We wonder, *Does God care?* And we become fearful because we don't know Jesus.

A while ago, I was confounded by a series of problems I faced as a pastor and parent. I wasn't wringing my hands, but I did have many anxious moments. I woke up at night, my mind churning over this bundle of challenges. What bothered me most about the situation was the fact that I knew I was demonstrating an Olympic lack of faith. I've learned a lot about peace since then, and I would like to pass on to you a little of what the Lord has taught me.

I've learned that not only is God love, but He is also peace. In at least seven places, the Bible identifies Him as the God of peace. We don't normally think of the words *God of peace* as one of His titles, but it is, and I believe it is a very important one. God doesn't bite His nails, nor does He pace the floor. He's never edgy, restless, or nervously wringing His hands. Just as God is always love, so, likewise, He is always peace.

The word *peace* is used about four hundred times in the Bible—which means it is an important theme. God has a lot to say about it. The Hebrew word translated as "peace" is *shalom.* In essence, *shalom* means peace, safety, well-being, happiness, friendliness, health, prosperity, and/or favor. The Greek word translated "peace" in the New Testament is *eirēnē.* (The name *Irene* is derived from this word.) It can mean peace, prosperity, quietness, rest, to set at one again, and/or to restore.[1] These are wonderful definitions, aren't they? They're sweet, inviting words. And the entire plan of salvation revolves around these words because in our lost condition we're alienated from God; we're at war against Him. But Jesus, who is the pure Prince of Peace, came to reconcile us. He came to make peace with the Father on our behalf because our sins have separated us from God.

Misconceptions of peace

People look for all kinds of peace. Many fear nuclear war; they want world peace so nations won't annihilate each other. But Jesus warned, "Think not that I am come to send peace on earth: I came not to send peace, but a sword" (Matthew 10:34,KJV). Wars and crusades have been fought in Jesus' name, so this can't be the peace He's offering.

People who are plagued by constant conflict in their homes long for domestic peace. Obtaining domestic peace is a blessing, but Jesus didn't come primarily to establish that kind of peace. In fact, He said, "I am come to set a man at variance against his father, and the daughter against her mother, and the daughter in law against her mother in law" (Matthew 10:35, KJV). The gospel of Christ can certainly bring peace into a divided home, but it can just as easily bring division.

Some people seek peace through financial security. Every day they anxiously check their stocks, and if the market goes up, they're elated; but when it drops, they're agitated. Who can have peace when they're living like that? And others are constantly fending off bill collectors. People who are drowning in debt don't have peace. Sometimes they think, *If I could just win the lottery, then I'd have peace.* But the Bible says the good things of life don't come from the abundance of things we possess (see Luke 12:15). Proverbs 11:28 says, "He that trusteth in his riches shall fall: but the righteous shall flourish as a branch" (KJV).

Still others look for peace in rituals or in cultlike religions, or, hopeless, they turn to drugs for the temporary feelings of peace they provide. The devil wants us to direct our pursuit of peace toward these popular counterfeits: secure finances, a quiet domestic life, physical health, and/or political calm. And many are deceived by these false forms of peace. But none of these are the kind of peace God promises. All these forms of peace change so quickly. Remember Job? He lost his financial security, physical health, and family serenity all at once.

So where can we find abiding peace that will give us rest no matter what our circumstances?

Authentic peace

I'm amazed when I read that Peter slept the night before his execution (see Acts 12). That's incredible! He had a peace that surpasses understanding. How would you like to find that kind of peace—one that keeps you from being anxious even though your life is on the line?

Martin Luther King Jr. said, "True peace is not merely the absence of some negative force—tension, confusion, or war; it is the presence of some positive force."[2] Ridding yourself of negative forces will provide peace only temporarily. Eventually, some other crisis will sprout to destroy your tranquility. You'll be constantly riding the roller coaster of peace and worry. True, abiding peace must come from an inner dynamic.

I once saw a bumper sticker that said, "No God, No peace; Know God, Know peace." That tells us the Source of true peace. It comes from knowing God. Job 22:21 says, "Acquaint now thyself with him, and be at peace" (KJV). How do we acquaint ourselves with God? Through communion with Him—through reading His Word. When we allow Him to speak to us, we'll find peace. Then we can have "the peace of God, which passeth all understanding, [that] shall keep your hearts and minds through Christ Jesus" (Philippians 4:7, KJV). He'll give us this peace when we begin to know Him. So, the real power of peace is found in the promises of God's Word. Christ met every one of Satan's temptations with that Word. Knowing Scripture gave Jesus the power and peace to overcome.

Embracing an attitude of gratitude can also provide us with great peace. Focus on those things for which you should be grateful—on what you have. Sometimes, we become agitated because we forget our blessings and ponder our problems. We become discontent by focusing on what is wrong or what we lack and we forget all the blessings we already have. We should thank God for what we have. Remember, Paul said that we should pray, we should supplicate, we should request, and then we should thank. When we thank the God of peace, He'll give us incredible contentment (see Philippians 4:6, 7).

Through Jesus, God will also guard our hearts and minds against the devil's attacks of distress, which are designed to destroy our peace. David said, "I will both lay me down in peace, and sleep: for thou, LORD, only makest me dwell in safety" (Psalm 4:8, KJV). Even though King Saul and an entire army were hunting David to kill him, he could sleep like a baby because he knew God was with him. Christians become the most effective witnesses to unbelievers when they retain their peace even while passing through trials. When we're going through a storm and yet are at peace, our witness draws others to God.

Most people are centered on self. Trying to find peace in that circumstance is like trying to find peace at the epicenter of an earthquake. We can have peace only when our world is centered on God. He's the calm in the eye of a hurricane. When we're in Him, the storm may be raging all around us, but within, all is still.

Meditation can bring us peace too. I don't mean transcendental meditation. Rather, the Bible tells us to meditate *on God*, to commune with Him in our hearts. We can do so through pondering His blessings, provision, and providence.

At my family's mountain cabin, we can see the panorama of a peaceful valley spread below us. A friend built us a beautiful oak bench swing that we've put on the upstairs porch. Karen, my wife, likes to spend time there just meditating or reading.

One day I began to feel restless because of unfinished projects that were piling up. But I looked at Karen, who was sitting in the swing, and I thought, *I need to try that!* So I joined her on the swing. As we rocked gently back and forth, I surveyed the meadows and the birds. Then I heard that still, small Voice, and suddenly, I found myself at peace. That's why the Bible tells us to be still and to know that He is God (see Psalm 46:10). If we behold God's creation, we'll find real rest.

Isaiah 26:3 says, "Thou wilt keep him in perfect peace, whose mind is stayed on thee: because he trusteth in thee" (KJV). That's true meditation—keeping our minds fixed on God. I like to call this condition a "calm-plex." When we stay our mind on God, we can have that healthy calm-plex.

I saw a sign in front of a church that said, "If life is a puzzle, look here for the missing peace." I agree that, along with reading the Word, meditating, praying, and exercising faith, a church environment can help us find peace. Peace can be contagious. We can learn much about the peace of God by fellowship with others who know the Prince of Peace.

Peace through obedience

Peace also comes through obedience—by surrendering to Him and by knowing we're in God's will. Philippians 4:9 says, "Those things, which ye have both learned, and received, and heard, and seen in me, do: and the God of peace shall be with you" (KJV). That's an important biblical message. "Mark the perfect man, and behold the upright: for the end of that man is peace" (Psalm 37:37, KJV).

Many people haven't realized the big connection between peace and obedience, but the Bible is clear: "Great peace have they which love thy law: and nothing shall offend them" (Psalm 119:165, KJV). In fact, when I counsel fretful souls, I usually ask, "Is there something you're doing that isn't in harmony with God's will?" Often they'll admit to being disobedient in some area of their life. God loves us too much to let us have peace while we're drifting towards destruction by disobeying our conscience and His will. Would you want your children to be at peace if they were disobeying you?

Jonah is a perfect example of this disobedience-tribulation syndrome. Jonah was running west when God had told him to go east. He soon found himself in the midst of a terrible storm. Jonah lost his peace when he acted directly against the known will of God. The Bible is full of similar stories and counsels that remind us of this principle. "The work of righteousness will be peace, and the effect of righteousness, quietness and assurance forever" (Isaiah 32:17). And "O that thou hadst hearkened to my commandments! then had thy peace been as a river" (Isaiah 48:18, KJV). Notice that Isaiah didn't say, "Your peace would have been like a creek." Do you know why? A creek dries up. But a river doesn't; it runs continually. A river may fall or rise some, but it always flows. It's constant. And God's peace just keeps on moving—it's always there, available, and ever flowing.

When I was fifteen years old, I stole some money from my employer. It wasn't much money—fifteen dollars—but my boss trusted me, and my theft always bothered me. Years later, after I was born again, the Holy Spirit impressed me, "Doug, you need to go and make it right." But I didn't want to, so I lost my peace. I tried to rationalize it: "Oh, that was twenty years ago, and it involved so little money." I had accepted

Christ, and God had forgiven me, so why was it bothering me?

I think it has to do with the fact that peace is progressive. To stay at peace, we must continually grow in God's will as He reveals new things to us. Many Christians have new truths revealed to them, but they say, "I don't want to follow that because it's different." And sure enough, before long they lose their peace! If God reveals new light to us, we can't refuse to walk in it.

Eventually, the Lord graced me with strength, and I returned to the place where I had worked. When I went in, my hands were sweating. Ironically, the employer from whom I stole the money was no longer there, and no one knew where he had gone. But I found my missing peace. You see, God didn't want my fifteen dollars. He wanted my willingness to make things right. And once I was in God's will for me, I had my peace back again. It was flowing like a river once more. "When peace, like a river, attendeth my way, . . . it is well with my soul."[3]

God invites us to be at peace, but He also wants us to be purveyors of peace—peacemakers. He wants us to share that peace with others. We can't keep it to ourselves because, like happiness, it's something we retain only by giving it away. Jesus said, "Blessed are the peacemakers, for they shall be called the sons of God" (Matthew 5:9).

How are we to be peacemakers? Is God calling us to become politicians with seats at the United Nations? Not particularly. As Christian peacemakers, we are to invite people to make peace with God. That's our foremost responsibility.

When Jesus commissioned His disciples to preach, He instructed them to say "Peace be to this house" when they entered a home (Luke 10:5, KJV). As we invite the Prince of

Peace into our hearts and become ambassadors to an anxious and fretful world, we are to communicate this benediction.

Why not now?

Do you long to find peace? Jesus entered the world with a proclamation of peace—the angels sang, "And on earth peace, goodwill toward men" (Luke 2:14). And He concluded His ministry the same way. Before ascending to heaven, He appeared to His disciples in the upper room and said, "Peace be unto you" (Luke 24:36, KJV). Ephesians 2:14, 15, 17 says this about our King: "He Himself is our peace, who has made both one, and has broken down the middle wall of separation, . . . thus making peace. . . . And He came and preached peace to you who were afar off and to those who were near." In our lost state, we are at war with God. But Jesus unites us to God. He brings peace among us and between us and the Father. No doubt that's why He's called the Prince of Peace.

A few years ago, my wife, Karen, and I went scuba diving in the Great Barrier Reef. We got caught in a storm on a small charter boat. The captain frankly told us and the other passengers that our lives were at risk. He then steered the boat behind a huge rock near an island. The storm raged around us that night, but as long as we were anchored behind that rock, we were sheltered from the gale and the waves, and we were able to sleep peacefully. During the night, the anchor slipped, and we were violently rocked awake. But the captain simply steered us behind the rock again, and it was calm once more.

This world is full of storms, but Jesus is our Rock; we'll find shelter only in Him. "Peace I leave with you," He says. "My peace I give to you; not as the world gives do I give to you" (John 14:27). God wants you to have peace! Not a peace that's dependent on political, social, physical, domestic, or financial circumstances, but an internal peace—the peace that God gives, not that which the world gives. Peace like a river. Peace that passes understanding.

I want you to have that kind of peace, a peace that no devil can steal. If you want it, you can have it through a trusting relationship with God, communion in prayer, fellowship with His people, immersing yourself in His Word, and surrendering to His will.

Now you know the Source of peace in this life. But an even better peace is sure to come. Someday, there will be nothing but total peace everywhere. Isaiah 11:6 promises "The wolf also shall dwell with the lamb, and the leopard shall lie down with the kid; and the calf and the young lion and the fatling together; and a little child shall lead them" (KJV). This means peace in creation, peace in our relationships, and peace in the whole world. It's simply waiting for you to claim it.

1. *Strong's Hebrew and Greek Dictionary.*

2. Martin Luther King Jr., *A Testament of Hope: The Essential Writings and Speeches of Martin Luther King, Jr.,* ed. James Washington (New York: HarperCollins, 1991), 6.

3. Horatio G. Spafford, "It Is Well With My Soul," in *Seventh-day Adventist Hymnal* (Hagerstown, Md.: Review and Herald®, 1985), no. 530.

Chapter 12
Where Are You Going?

They desire a better, that is, a heavenly country.
Therefore God is not ashamed
to be called their God, for He has prepared a city for them.
—Hebrews 11:16

Between March 1999 and March 2000, 43.4 million Americans moved.[1] That's about 15 percent of our population! Where is everyone going?

In exploring who we think we really are, it's important to have a clear picture of two matters: First, where we have come from. We looked at this in chapter 1. Second, we also—and especially—need to know where we're going. If we're re-created in the image of God and adopted into His family, then heaven must be our homeland.

Someone once said, "A fugitive is someone running from home. A vagabond has no home. A stranger is someone who is away from home. And a pilgrim is someone who is in a strange land but who's on his way home."

An Easterner was being driven by a rancher friend over a long, blistering, and almost barren stretch of west Texas when a large, brightly colored bird scurried across the road in front of them. The visitor asked what kind of bird it was. "That's a bird-of-paradise," said the rancher. "Pretty long way from home, isn't it!" remarked the visitor.

Pilgrims get homesick for their homes and their native country. It's important for believers to remember that this world is not our home and when we are saved, we receive a new, celestial nationality. "Our citizenship is in heaven, from which we also eagerly wait for the Savior, the Lord Jesus Christ" (Philippians 3:20). "Here we have no continuing city, but we seek the one to come" (Hebrews 13:14).

Bring my bones home

My dad was born in Oklahoma. His early life there was pretty tough. He traveled to California when he was fifteen, along with thousands of other dust bowl migrants. Dad never returned to live in Oklahoma, spending the rest of his eighty-three years in California and Florida. That's why it's a little odd that when he made plans for his burial, he purchased a plot back in Oklahoma. That's where he's buried today. Something within all of us yearns for a rest in the place of our nativity.

According to the dictionary, a *home* is "an environment offering security and happiness"; "a valued place regarded as a refuge or place of origin"; "the place, such as a country or town, where one was born or has lived for a long period."[2] It has been said, "Home is a place where the great are small, and the small are great." Someone else described *home* as "a place where you can find your way around in the dark." Within all of us is a longing to rest in a place that is secure and familiar. Virtually everyone gathers some of their identity from their national roots.

When the famous missionary and explorer David Livingstone died, his friends Chuma and Susi buried his heart under a tree in Africa, as he had requested. They then embalmed his body by filling it with salt and leaving it to dry in the sun for fourteen days. They wrapped it in cloth, enclosed it in the bark of a myonga tree, and sewed heavy sailcloth over it all. Then they tied this odd package to a long pole so that two men could carry it.

Then Chuma and Susi started on a dangerous and epic eleven-month, thousand-mile journey to Zanzibar. (Talk about friendship!) When they arrived in February 1874, they gave Livingstone's body to the amazed officers of the British Consul, who shipped it to England. On April 18, 1874, virtually all of London came to a standstill as Livingstone's remains were buried in Westminster Abbey.

As you may have guessed, this saga reminds me of a Bible hero whose embalmed body was carried to the Promised Land, to be buried there. "Joseph took an oath from the children of Israel, saying, 'God will surely visit you, and you shall carry up my bones from here' " (Genesis 50:25). His bones were hand carried for more than forty years and one thousand miles before he was finally buried in the Promised Land. Both Joseph and David Livingstone lived and worked is a foreign land, and both of them wanted to be buried in their homeland. Both believed in the resurrection, and they wanted to wake up at home.

Do you long for home? Are you missing that rest for which all weary pilgrims yearn? We can find it when we come to Jesus. He said, "Come to Me, all you who labor and are heavy laden, and I will give you rest" (Matthew 11:28). Those who follow Him have no permanent dwelling on this earth. Even the Creator saw Himself as a wandering alien in this lost world. "Foxes have holes and birds of the air have nests, but the Son of Man has nowhere to lay His head," He said (Luke 9:58).

In the nineteenth century, people who passed the Rothschild mansion in a fashionable quarter of London noticed that the end of one of the pieces of exterior molding was unfinished. Many wondered why the richest man in the world didn't have that part of the wall finished. Was it due to carelessness or stinginess? It wasn't. The explanation is very simple. Lord Rothschild was an orthodox Jew, and tradition says the house of every pious Jew must not be completely finished—to bear testimony to the world that its occupant is only, like Abraham, a pilgrim and a stranger upon the earth.

According to a famous saying, "Home is where the heart is." Perhaps that's why Ruth was willing to cancel her citizenship in Moab and move to Bethlehem. Her love for Naomi was stronger then her patriotism. Ruth made one of the most beautiful declarations of loyalty to be found in Scripture. She said, "Intreat me not to leave thee, or to return from following after thee: for whither thou goest, I will go; and where thou lodgest, I will lodge: thy people shall be my people, and thy God my God: where thou diest, will I die, *and there will I be buried:* the LORD do so to me, and more also, if ought but death part thee and me" (Ruth 1:16, 17, KJV; emphasis added).

On the tenth of April 1852, beneath the African sun, an American died. He was laid to rest in a lonely cemetery in Tunis. Thirty-one years later, as an act of a grateful public, the United States dispatched a man-of-war ship to the African coast. American hands opened that grave, reverently placed the remains of the man's body on board the battleship, and turned again for his native land.

Their arrival in an American harbor was saluted by the firing of guns in the fort and by a display of flags at half-mast. The man's casket was carried to the nation's capital city on a special train. There was a suspension of all business, an adjournment of all departments of government, and, as the funeral procession passed down Pennsylvania Avenue, the president, vice president, members of the cabinet, congressmen, judges of the Supreme Court, officers of the army and navy, and a mass of private citizens, rich and poor, stood with uncovered heads.

To whom did they pay this unprecedented respect? To a man who simply expressed the yearning of his heart for the domestic tranquility of a pious home and expressed that longing in the words of the song "Home, Sweet Home"

'Mid pleasures and palaces though we may roam,
Be it ever so humble, there's no place like home.
—John Howard Payne

If in God's providence you must be laid to rest in this foreign land before the coming of Christ, do not ever fear that He will forget to wake you up and bring you home. The resources of a grateful nation were mobilized to bring home the author of this song. But all heaven will work to get you home.

A tree or a turnip?

You've probably heard the joke about a commercial aircraft that was flying across the Atlantic and ran into a lightning storm. After a while, the pilot came on the public address system and said, "Well, folks, I have some good news, and I have some bad news. First, the bad news: a half hour ago a bolt of lightning tagged our aircraft, and we lost all of our navigation equipment. We have absolutely no idea where we are. The good news is that we appear to be making excellent time."

You are moving and changing whether or not you know it. Nothing stands still. Every human is on the conveyor belt of time, and we can't get off. The question, of course, is, What direction are you moving? What are you becoming? What we do with our time here will determine our eternal destiny.

Here's another strange but important question: Are you a tree or a turnip?

Let me explain. Trees can be living monuments. The oldest

living tree, called Methuselah, is a bristlecone pine in California's White Mountains. It is estimated to be more than forty-seven hundred years old. The tallest living tree in the world is a redwood in Mendocino County, California. It stands 367 feet, 6 inches tall. That's five stories higher than the Statue of Liberty. And the most massive living thing on earth is a sequoia tree in Sequoia National Park in California. It's called the General Sherman. It's only 275 feet tall, but it weighs an estimated 2,145 tons, has a girth of 79 feet, and is estimated to be between 2,300 and 2,700 years old.

Then there are turnips. They're small and have a very short lifespan—one measured in weeks. Then they wither, crack, and die.

Do you approach life like a tree or turnip? Some people are always in a frenzy, convinced that life is a brief shopping spree. They run around eating and drinking and trying to get as much carnal pleasure as possible, believing that we're here for only a short while. Is that who you are?

Or are you like a tree—an ageless bristlecone pine? What does the Bible say? "As the days of a tree, so shall be the days of My people, and My elect shall long enjoy the work of their hands" (Isaiah 65:22).

Allow me to illustrate. If you were to win a ten-minute shopping spree at an electronics superstore, would you shop casually or as fast as possible? Of course, you'd be running at breakneck speed up and down the aisles, stuffing the most expensive items you can find into the shopping cart! You'd be in a frenzy. Why? Because you're thinking we're like turnips—our time is short. If all we see to life is the temporary pleasures of the here and now, we'll frantically try to grab as much of it as possible, all the while never realizing that this life is really about getting a good foundation for living in eternity. But

God wants us to experience life like a bristlecone pine tree, not a turnip. This brief life is not all there is!

Many years ago, a friend of mine worked in a newspaper office. One day he was sent to a home to get a photograph of a sixteen-year-old boy who had just been killed—shot on the street. Sixteen years old!

My friend felt kind of sheepish, coming to a house in mourning to ask for a picture. What he remembers most was, at one point, an older brother, who had been talking about the death of his troubled younger sibling, yelled out in front of my friend, "All that for nothing!"

All that for nothing?

Or what about the old man in China who was killed by a boiler that blew up, shot through the sky, and landed on his head? Was his life for nothing too?

What about *any* of us? We're here fifty, sixty, eighty years—maybe more if we wear helmets when we bike and avoid greasy foods and exploding boilers. But in the end, we're all on this inescapable conveyor belt to the cemetery. "We can take precautions against all sorts of things," wrote an ancient Greek named Epicurus, "but so far as death is concerned, we all of us live like the inhabitants of a defenseless citadel." Or, as someone else once said, "In the end, we're all dead anyway."

So, what do we do with our brief time here? How are we to understand ourselves and the meaning of our lives when at best they last eighty or ninety years, and at worst they can be snuffed out in some untimely sickness or accident? Your answer will affect your philosophy about everything else. Some Christians say they believe in heaven, judgment, and eternity, but in their innermost souls they're thinking like turnips "just in case." They're frantic because they think their brief life is slipping away with the ticking of the clock.

Who do you think you are? If you're like them, you'll always be frenzied because this life is indeed short. But if you believe you're like a tree, living with the promise of everlasting life, you won't feel driven to experience all your pleasures here and now. You'll be satisfied living with self-denial because you know even greater things await in Paradise. Remember, the psalmist promised, "At [His] right hand are pleasures forevermore" (Psalm 16:11)—all through eternity.

We don't have to think we're like turnips and we have to get all the pleasures of life crammed in our shopping cart right now. We can think, live, and plan as though we're trees. The one who trusts in the Lord is "like a tree planted by the rivers of water, that bringeth forth his fruit in his season; his leaf also shall not wither; and whatsoever he doeth shall prosper" (Psalm 1:3, KJV).

True, this world is temporary—but we don't have to be.

"I'm going home"

Thomas Wolfe said, "You can't go home again." But that isn't always true, and it certainly hasn't stopped many from trying. Who you think you are will be determined somewhat by where you think you're going and how focused you are on getting there.

Take Lillian Alling, for instance. In the spring of 1927, this young Russian immigrant living in New York City became very homesick and decided to return to her family in Russia. After two unhappy years among the crowds, she knew that life in the noisy city wasn't for her. Lillian wasn't able to afford passage across the Atlantic, but still, all she could think about was going home. So this young slip of a woman chose to walk across two continents back to her former home in Russia!

Supplied with hand-drawn maps, an iron pipe for protection, and a few dollars, she began her epoch journey. As she was very timid, she refused to accept rides from strangers, but still she averaged thirty to forty miles a day. Eventually, the frail girl passed through Chicago and on to Winnipeg, where the really tough part of her journey began. Keep in mind that back in 1927, there were few roads in that part of Canada. Except for the odd trading post or telegraph station, there was nothing but an unbroken stretch of the world's toughest terrain and wilderness. Even experienced mountain men thought twice about tackling this rough country alone.

But Lillian walked on day after day, across Saskatchewan, Alberta, and British Columbia. When she came to a swollen stream, she would float across clinging to a log. She slept in the open, enduring untold hardships and surviving on a meager diet of bread and wild berries. When asked where she was heading her firm reply was, "I'm going home to Russia. Please don't try to stop me."

When she reached Vancouver, her ragged condition and lack of provisions caused great concern among the locals. To prevent her from continuing on during the winter, she was arrested for vagrancy and thrown in jail. She used the several weeks she was held in the prison to regain her strength, and when spring arrived, she resumed her daunting quest, hiking across the Yukon next. Telegraph station operators kept track of her progress and gave her a few clothes and a dog. She wept when she learned that one telegrapher died in a blizzard while searching for her.

Lillian spent part of another winter in Dawson City, Yukon Territory, and arrived in Nome, Alaska, in July 1929. But this was only the halfway mark of her epic journey. She was last seen rowing a boat from Cape Prince of Wales across the thirty-six turbulent miles of the Bering Strait to Siberia.[3]

Did Lillian make it home? One man claimed he saw a woman on the Siberian coast in the fall of 1930. She was telling an astonished policeman that she'd walked all the way from New York. I sure hope it's true and that Lillian made it home and lived a long and happy life.

We marvel at Lillian Alling's incredible, tenacious determination to get to her humble home in Russia. How that contrasts with all the people who are indifferent about reaching the mansions Jesus has prepared for them in heaven. We need more resolve!

Total commitment

Dr. Bob Moorehead jotted down a personal pledge of determination to follow Jesus that I found inspiring.

I am part of the "Fellowship of the Unashamed." I have Holy Spirit power. The die has been cast. I've stepped over the line. The decision has been made. I am a disciple of His. I won't look back, let up, slow down, back away, or be still. My past is redeemed, my present makes sense, and my future is secure. I am finished and done with low living, sight walking, small planning, smooth knees, colorless dreams, tame visions, mundane talking, chintzy giving, and dwarfed goals!

I no longer need preeminence, prosperity, position, promotions, plaudits, or popularity. I don't have to be right, first, tops, recognized, praised, regarded, or rewarded. I now live by presence, learn by faith, love by patience, live by prayer, and labor by power.

My face is set, my gait is fast, my goal is heaven, my road is narrow, my way is rough, my companions few, my guide reliable, my mission clear. I cannot be bought, compromised, detoured, lured away, turned back, diluted, or delayed. I will not flinch in the face of sacrifice, hesitate in the presence of adversity, negotiate at the table of the enemy, ponder at the pool of popularity, or meander in the maze of mediocrity.

I won't give up, shut up, let go, or slow up until I've preached up, prayed up, paid up, stored up, and stayed up for the cause of Christ.

I am a disciple of Jesus. I must go till He comes, give till I drop, preach till all know, and work till He stops.

And when He comes to get His own, He'll have no problems recognizing me . . . my colors will be clear.[4]

A father took his young son to the local pound to pick out a puppy for his birthday. After reviewing a row of bouncing, barking inmates, the boy settled on a little mongrel puppy whose tail was wagging furiously.

"Why do you want that one?" the father inquired.

"Because he has a happy ending," the boy replied.

In running the Christian race, it is much more important that you have a good ending than a good beginning. Every butterfly was first a worm. A diamond begins as a lump of coal. David started as a backward shepherd but finished as a glorious king.

The key to a successful finish is to keep focused on the goal. You may slip at the starting line or stumble along the way, but what matters in the race of life is that you get up and end well. Paul said, "One thing I do, forgetting those things which are behind and reaching forward to those things which are ahead, I press toward the goal for the prize of the upward call of God in Christ Jesus" (Philippians 3:13, 14).

Are you packed?

In 1914, Sir Ernest Shackleton and his crew sailed to Antarctica, intending to cross the continent on foot. But before they reached Antarctica, their ship, the *Endurance,* became trapped in the ice and was crushed beyond repair. The stranded men camped on ice floes for almost a year and then paddled lifeboats to a small, rocky, desolate spit of land called Elephant Island.

Knowing that his crew would never survive the winter there, Shackleton took a few men and set off in a small boat on a treacherous, eight-hundred-mile journey to South Georgia Island to get help from a whaling station there. Before leaving his frozen friends marooned, he promised, "I will come back," and said, "Make sure you're packed!"

The courageous explorer kept his word. After miraculously finding a path through the ice, he and his little crew crossed the world's most hazardous ocean in their small lifeboat. Braving monstrous waves and hurricane winds, they reached the remote whaling station.

In spite of his hunger and exhaustion, Shackleton turned right back around with a rescue ship and returned for his stranded men. It was an epic journey through formidable barriers of ice. At the risk of losing the ship, his life, and the lives of his crew, he fought his way back to Elephant Island. Just when the death of the men stranded there from starvation and cold seemed imminent, he was able to reach and rescue them. And miraculously, not a single man was lost during the entire two-year ordeal.

When the whole party was on the rescue boat, out of the danger zone, and heading for home, Shackleton asked one of the rescued men: "Well, you were packed and ready, weren't you?"

"Yes, boss," came the reply. "We never lost hope. You had promised to return, and we believed somehow you would."[5]

Jesus won't leave His people stranded in this cold, desolate world. Our Master has promised, "I will come again" (see John 14:1–3). And no matter how impossible the fulfillment of this promise may seem at times, we are never to lose hope. Nothing will turn Jesus from His purpose to liberate the people He ransomed with His own life and to bring them safely home. And nothing should be more important to us than being ready for His return.

Friend, are you packed? Do you have your priorities in order—seeking first His kingdom and His righteousness? Do you know where you've come from, what you're doing here, and where you're going? Do you know how much you are worth to the King of kings—what He has paid to adopt and redeem you? Do you know who you really are?

I trust you do, but if you don't, why not ask Him right now. In prayer, entrust your life this moment to the Captain of your salvation. He's waiting.

1. U.S. Bureau of the Census, *Geographic Mobility: March 1999 to March 2000,* prepared by Jason Schachter (Washington, D.C.: U.S. Bureau of the Census, May 2001).

2. *American Heritage Dictionary of the English Language*, 4th ed., s.v. "Home."

3. Calvin Rutstrum, *The Way of the Wilderness* (n. p.: Burgess Publishing, 1946).

4. Bob Moorehead, *Words Aptly Spoken* (Redmond, Wash.: Overlake Christian Press, 1995), 99, quoted in Bill and Lynne Hybels, *Rediscovering Church* (Grand Rapids, Mich.: Zondervan, 1995), 194; ellipses in original.

5. Alfred Lansing, *Endurance: Shackleton's Incredible Voyage* (New York: Carroll & Graf Publishers, 1986).

Amazing *Bible Studies*

that could

Change your *Life!*

Our **Bible Study Guides** are easy to read and relevant for today's world!

Log on today and discover:

- What happens after death
- The way to better health
- How to save your marriage
- The truth about hell fire and many other amazing facts!

Go online at

www.amazingfacts.org

OR   8326

Send for the printed guides absolutely **FREE!**

Name _____

Address _____

PLEASE PRINT CLEARLY

City _____

State _____ ZIP _____

Free offer available in North America and U.S. territories only.